1982

THE SEVENTH ALFRED I. duPONT-COLUMBIA UNIVERSITY SURVEY OF BROADCAST JOURNALISM

THE ALFRED I. duPONT–COLUMBIA UNIVERSITY SURVEY AND AWARDS IN BROADCAST JOURNALISM

THE JURORS

Osborn Elliott, chairman
Michael Arlen
Richard T. Baker

Edward W. Barrett
Dorothy Height
Michael Novak

Marvin Barrett, director

Barbara Murray Eddings, assistant director

Harry Arouh and Carolyn Lewis, special consultants

THE SEVENTH ALFRED I. duPONT-
COLUMBIA UNIVERSITY

SURVEY OF
BROADCAST
JOURNALISM

THE EYE OF THE STORM

MARVIN BARRETT & ZACHARY SKLAR

LIPPINCOTT & CROWELL, PUBLISHERS
NEW YORK

FIRST EDITION

Designed by Ginger Legato

U.S. Library of Congress Cataloging in Publication Data

Barrett, Marvin.
    The eye of the storm.

    (The Seventh Alfred I. duPont-Columbia University survey of broadcast journalism)
    Includes index.
    1. Television broadcasting of news—United States.   I. Sklar, Zachary, joint author.
II. Title.   III. Series: Alfred I. Du Pont Foundation. Alfred I. Du Pont-Columbia University survey of broadcast journalism; 7th.
PR4784.T4A43   7th [PR4888.T4]   791.45'5
ISBN 0-690-01876-2   80-11379
ISBN 0-690-01916-5 (pbk.)

80 81 82 83 84 10 9 8 7 6 5 4 3 2 1

Contents

Foreword

The Eye of the Storm, the latest Alfred I. duPont–
Columbia University Survey of Broadcast Journalism,
goes to press just ten years after the first volume of this
ongoing series appeared. The decade 1969–1979, covered in seven books and three interim reports, has
unquestionably been the most tumultuous in the short,
lively history of broadcasting. And it was in the news
and public affairs sector that the greatest excitement
lay.

The current volume, by marking the industry's
course through the past ten years, aims to give some
indication of the direction in which the formidable enterprise of electronic journalism is heading. Between
the seasons of 1968–69 and 1978–79, annual network
news budgets more than tripled. TV news directors'
salaries climbed by well over 50 percent in the seven
years from 1972 to 1979. The average for top staff TV
news personnel shot up by more than 90 percent, with
no ceiling yet on what a popular anchorperson could
command.

From being a loss leader, news has become one of

broadcasting's biggest money-makers. A top-rated newscast is a prime indication of success both locally and nationwide.

Meanwhile, television's popularity as the nation's primary news source has climbed steadily, standing first with 51 percent in 1959 and with 67 percent according to the latest Roper poll for 1978. Audiences for the three TV network newscasts, estimated at slightly more than 35 million in 1968, had grown to more than 47 million by November 1978. Among all media, TV news rated first in credibility, leading newspapers two to one. And this approval was not undeserved.

The same ten years that saw the growth in budgets, income, and audiences brought a similar growth in scope and expertise among radio and TV news personnel. In the first year of the DuPont-Columbia Awards, 200 examples of broadcast journalism were rated of sufficient interest to be considered by the jurors. Last year the number had grown to 1,300, and the quality of submissions, particularly from individual stations, had dramatically improved.

And yet, frustration has figured almost as frequently as enthusiasm in the reports from the growing grid of DuPont-Columbia correspondents and the hundreds of local and network newspeople who have from year to year contributed their carefully considered opinions to the Survey.

At the outset of the 1968–69 broadcast season, the first that the DuPont-Columbia Survey assessed, Julian Goodman, then president of the National Broadcasting Company and a former newsman himself, greeted his affiliates with these words:

> I see broadcasting faced by a troubling and frustrating paradox. Our media have become the most

important sources of news and information to most of the public. Yet I can't remember a time when we have been under such critical attack or been viewed with such suspicion and distrust, by so many who, on the merits of our case, should be our friends. . . . Above all, we should strive to operate in a fashion that is above reproach by even our narrowest and most demanding critics. This means reaching for a higher degree of excellence and a deeper commitment to public service. It requires care and thoughtfulness in everything we do. There is no room for timidity, but there is great need for experiment and innovation.

Goodman's advice was put to the test time after time in the succeeding decade. Sometimes the test was passed with flying colors, at other times the colors dipped a bit.

During that same period, the Survey has taken its place among the medium's growing body of critical observers and admirers.

We are grateful for the foresight of the Alfred I. du-Pont Awards Foundation, particularly Jessie Ball du-Pont, in perceiving the continuing importance of broadcast journalism and making it possible for us to honor its best expressions as well as chronicle its unfolding story.

Marvin Barrett, Director

Part I:

The More It Changes: A Decade of Broadcast Journalism

November 13, 1969, the publication date of the first DuPont-Columbia Survey, coincided with an event of some importance in the history of broadcast journalism. It was on that day, at 6:00 P.M. Central Standard Time, from the grand ballroom of the Hotel Fort Des Moines in Des Moines, Iowa, that Spiro T. Agnew, then vice-president of the United States, preempted the evening newscasts on all three commercial networks to tell the men who had provided him with his rostrum that they were doing a lousy job.

It was a speech intended not only to criticize but to intimidate, and there were many in the business of broadcast news who felt that—thanks to the Vice-President's position of power and the vulnerability of their licensed industry to government attack—broadcast journalism would never be the same again. Others in the administration joined in the attacks, which became both more emphatic and specific, and support ran better than three to one in favor of Agnew among the 238,000 people who made their opinions known to the networks and Washington.

But time proved that anxiety on the part of the

11

broadcasters, at least those broadcasters Agnew cared most about—the commercial networks and their affiliates—was unwarranted. After one or two nervous parries, Vice-President Agnew's main target, the "tiny, enclosed fraternity of privileged men elected by no one and enjoying a monopoly sanctioned and licensed by government," closed ranks.

Shortly thereafter, broadcast journalists were standing witness to—indeed hastening—the departure of not only Agnew but most of his associates in office, including the President himself. The broadcasters' performance, reluctant though it was at the outset, became the most vivid possible proof that the Vice-President's estimate of their power was, if anything, below the mark.

Late on the scene or not, broadcasters had in Watergate their story of the decade. With the help of microphone and camera, all possibilities seemed explored, contradictions finally resolved. And if the punishments meted out were deemed inappropriate by some, the evidence upon which they were based, thanks largely to TV and radio, was there for everyone to examine.

Most surprising of all was the demonstration that the public could tolerate such massive exposure. Unfortunately, this proof that American listeners and viewers were willing and able to pay attention to important matters was ignored or immediately forgotten by too many of the nation's broadcasting executives. Entertainment once more took precedence over information. Still, at the end of the decade the impact of Watergate was acknowledged as lasting and important. Two thirds of the 350 working newspeople reporting to the Survey this year gave Watergate credit for an increased pride in their vocation and for a renewed respect and support from management and the public. Two comments were typical. From Louisiana:

> "Remember Watergate" ought to be a slogan for reporters forever. The most powerful political figure on earth used all the power he could muster to try to silence the press. He failed. The press pursued. The President resigned. What greater lesson could there be of the need for journalists to be tenacious, strong, thorough? Watergate was the greatest journalistic triumph of the twentieth century. At this one small television station in southern Louisiana, Watergate keeps us digging.

From Agnew's home state of Maryland:

> It is my personal opinion that broadcast journalism remains the only potent force toward maintaining freedom in America. The Watergate episode continues as a major influence in most broadcast newsrooms, especially when dealing with politicians and big business.

The other big stories of the decade were not so readily accommodated or clearly communicated by radio and TV. Vietnam, with its beginnings far in the past, played itself out on the tube in a fragmentary, confusing, and deeply disturbing way. The coverage it received from TV was enough to justify its label as the "living room war," another example of the power, however inadvertent, of the medium. And caught in the daily flow into the nation's parlors were striking individual passages, including Mike Wallace's devastating interviews with Private Paul Meadlo and Captain Ernest Medina concerning the massacre at My Lai, and John Laurence's *CBS Evening News* series on what the war was like for one company of grunts in the field.

These and dozens of other painful splinters of the truth penetrated the minds of Americans, carrying with them the uncomfortable suspicion that we were somewhere we shouldn't be and our presence there was having a terrible effect not only on "them" but on "us."

Unlike Vietnam, civil rights was a struggle that had no perceivable end—and the broadcaster's part in reminding Americans of this continuing crisis at home was crucial. Following the coverage of the stirring and agonizing events of the 1960s, it became a matter of pointing out to viewers that an enormous job remained to be done and that what had apparently already been achieved was in continual need of reinforcement. Throughout the decade, some of the most eloquent journalism, local and network, had to do with the fight for racial justice.

Here local stations frequently equaled and sometimes outclassed the networks in the sensitivity and effectiveness of their coverage. At the beginning of the decade, there was WBZ Radio's remarkable sensitivity session that closeted black militants with Boston's arch-conservative Louise Day Hicks for twenty-five straight hours, as well as KNXT Los Angeles's "Black on Black," Group W's "Oakland: A Tale of Two Cities," NET's "Trial: The City and County of Denver vs. Lauren R. Watson," Diane Orr's "Warrior Without a Weapon" for KUTV Salt Lake City, Tony Batten's "Youth Gangs in the South Bronx" for WNET, and John Drimmer's "Towers of Frustration" for WNJT. At the end of the decade the coverage was no less necessary and eloquent, as evidenced by such programs as KENS San Antonio's "And Justice for All," WFAA Dallas's "Race Relations: Where Are We Now?" and WTMJ Milwaukee's three-hour "A Human Relations Test."

Throughout the decade, as community after community underwent the ordeal of desegregation and busing, the local broadcasters were continually trying to reassure the timid and demonstrate to the intransigent what indeed was possible. Among the cities particularly well served by the local stations in this regard were Rochester, New York; Charlotte, North Carolina; Kansas City, Missouri; and Louisville, Kentucky.

The year 1969 saw the trajectory of space coverage reach its apogee with the landing on the moon, which provided the single most striking sequence of images of the century, perhaps in recorded history. Almost as startling was the quick falling-off of public interest once the unattainable had been attained. By the end of the 1970s, TV was paying only the most casual heed to the fly-bys of Jupiter and Saturn as the Voyager rockets sent back their amazing messages across the solar system.

As the decade unrolled, a similar offhandedness threatened to dull the public's reaction to deeds of senseless violence. After the shocking murders of Martin Luther King, Jr., and Robert F. Kennedy, and the uproar at the Democratic Convention in Chicago, a seemingly unending series of riots, hijackings, and acts of terrorism unfolded—Kent State, Munich, the SLA, Attica, the Baader-Meinhof Gang, the Red Brigade, the South Moluccans, the Hanafi Muslims. The bloody sequence reinforced the uneasy suspicion that society was out of control and that the media not only bore primary witness to the fact but was in some mysterious, ill-defined way responsible for it. Concerted efforts were made by networks and individual stations to ensure against this alarming possibility, and still, ten years later, the insane bloodletting continued, reaching the height of mindless horror during the season just past with the mass suicides and murders at Jonestown. In that appalling event, which was precipitated by reporter Don Harris's persistent on-camera grilling of the psychotic cult leader Jim Jones, the media's involvement was there up front for all to see and ponder.

How "responsible" was broadcast journalism, and how did it affect the painful matters it chose to report? These remained two of the enigmas of the decade, as far from solution at the end as at the beginning.

Nowhere was this odd reciprocation of cause and effect, this entangling of ends with means, more apparent than in TV's relationships to affluence and the spoliation that seemed to accompany it.

Two fairly straightforward examples of television becoming its own target were singled out by the Du-Pont-Columbia jurors this past season: WCCO-TV Minneapolis' "A Death in the Family," which held the phenomenon of compulsive televiewing up to uncomfortable scrutiny, and the CBS *60 Minutes* segment "The Ratings Game," which questioned the whole basis of network TV programming.

Despite broadcasting's obvious involvement in our society's psychic troubles, and its sometimes dangerous indifference to them, the men and women of television and radio, to their credit, continued to explore those areas where they themselves and their employers could be most justifiably called to account.

It had been eight years since Robert Markowitz's excruciating essay for CBS on the woes of the prosperous in Birmingham, Michigan, ". . . But What If the Dream Comes True?"; seven years since the TV audience had made the uncomfortable acquaintance of the Loud family in twelve hours of exposure on the Public Broadcasting Service; six years since Fred Freed profiled San Jose, the fastest-growing community in California, in "But Is This Progress?" And still the subject of the wages of affluence exercised its perennial fascination. One of the most bitterly controversial programs of the past year was "I Want It All Now," a revelation of the miseries of some of the most economically blessed inhabitants on the globe—the residents of Marin County, across the Golden Gate Bridge from San Francisco—already tellingly exposed two seasons before in Paul Wilkes's award-winning "Six American Families."

The advanced technological society of which broadcasting is so conspicuous a component had other, harsher effects to be reported. In 1965 *CBS Reports'* "Bulldozed America" struck an early ominous note. By 1968, when the Survey began its observations, this note was sounding louder and stronger in such efforts as Don Widener's "The Slow Guillotine," a local documentary of network caliber that dealt with the effects of air pollution in and around the Los Angeles basin.

Year by year the decibel level rose in such eloquent network and local statements as Fred Freed's *NBC White Paper* on "Pollution Is a Matter of Choice" and WOOD-TV Grand Rapids' "Our Poisoned World" (both 1970), "Timetable for Disaster," "A Sea of Trouble," and "Powers That Be," all by Don Widener for KNBC Los Angeles in 1970–71, and Dick Hubert and Group W's ". . . And the Rich Shall Inherit the Earth" (1973). Particularly ominous was the sequence of essays covering the growth and proliferation of nuclear power, including such programs as *Nova*'s "Incident at Brown's Ferry," Joan Konner's "Danger: Radioactive Wastes" for NBC, and Don Widener's "Plutonium: An Element of Risk" for KCET Los Angeles.

Coverage of the atomic era and its attendant problems reached full volume during the past season in such individual documentaries as PBS' "Paul Jacobs and the Nuclear Gang" and KUTV Salt Lake City's "Clouds of Doubt," climaxing in the massive coverage of Three Mile Island (see chapter 8).

And the items clustered around Three Mile Island and the nuclear industry were only the loudest of a host of warnings sounded by broadcast journalists in the past year about what Americans breathed, consumed, and lived next door to. How personally and deeply involved the media had become was demonstrated at one extreme by Paul Jacobs, who saw his own death as a sacrifice to his twenty-year pursuit of the truth about nuclear fallout and low-level radiation, and at the other by the continuing struggle between the media and the business community, which centered around the coverage of energy, environment, and public health. This struggle involved most of broadcasting's sponsors and many of its proprietors.

Resistance to and obstruction of the coverage of these sensitive topics was reported in no fewer than 180 separate instances by news personnel communicating to the Survey during the past season, the highest incidence of such protests in the history of the Survey —this despite the fact that only twenty stations had expressed an editorial position against nuclear energy and forty-two had reported editorial support for nuclear technology. One hundred forty-three respondents found hostility toward their news and public affairs operations had increased, again the largest number in the history of the Survey to admit this hazard. Among the comments:

> Our most recurring problem here is the technological complexity of these topics. We are report-

ers, not engineers and scientists. Too often we have to rely on the technical expertise of people involved in controversies. Too often we do little more than establish a forum for "pro" and "con" experts to disagree. Resistance has not been a major problem, however.

Charlotte, North Carolina

With energy, there is difficulty. With pollution, there is resistance. In the case of energy, the difficulty, quite candidly, is our own ignorance. Most reporters are abjectly ignorant of the complexities of the world energy situation, as well as its economics, logistics, and political intricacies. In the case of pollution, the resistance on the part of the exposed offender is understandable.

New Orleans, Louisiana

In the case of energy and pollution, the special interest pressures are a hindrance to objectivity. The major utility in our area has lost (so far) approval for a nuclear power plant, and tries very hard to influence coverage. Protestors are not quite as sophisticated, but continue to stage media events. Companies accused of pollution are seldom willing to tell their side of the story because they assume the news media are biased against business.

Eau Claire, Wisconsin

Experiencing difficulty or resistance is an integral part of the nature and challenge of journalism. We expect it and surmount it. The difficulty or resistance almost invariably takes the form of locating good sources, obtaining and verifying information.

San Francisco, California

The paradoxical miseries of the world's and history's richest nation were perhaps most clearly exposed in that primary staple of broadcast fare—fiction and nonfiction—crime. Crime certainly brought out the worst in broadcasting in its day-by-day exploitation on both the news and entertainment segments of the schedule. Occasionally it called forth the very best in the courage and outspokenness of its treatment. In ten years of awards, nearly a third of those programs cited for excellence dealt with the causes and effects of crime. At the beginning of the decade, it was John Sharnik's three-part "Justice in America," Martin Carr's heartbreaking "This Child Is Rated X," and Geraldo Rivera's revealing "Drug Crisis in East Harlem," followed by such outstanding jobs as Richard Thurston Watkins's "Attica: The Unanswered Questions," Tex Fuller's "Murder One," and Susan and Alan Raymond's "The Police Tapes." During the past season, ABC's sixty-minute *Closeup*, "Arson: Fire for Hire" and KQED San Francisco's grueling "Tattooed Tears," surely the final word on man's inhumanity to incarcerated man, stood at the top of a pyramid of devastating examples of America's failure to properly inhibit, apprehend, judge, punish, and rehabilitate the nation's malefactors.

There were other victims of the affluent society that broadcasters continued to remind us of throughout the decade. No one caught the plight of these victims more eloquently than Frederick Wiseman, who won his first DuPont-Columbia Award in 1970 with his stunning "Hospital," a portrait of a big-city institution which was a microcosm of the small successes and broad failures of so many of the nation's do-good enterprises.

Other examples of Wiseman's reportorial and editorial skill, which have for many years topped the list of public TV's documentary offerings, included "Law and Order," "Primate," "Juvenile Court," "Welfare," "Canal Zone," and "Essene." Wiseman's career was further remarkable for the consistency of his output over the decade, an unusual characteristic in what had proved to be a highly volatile profession. Few TV documentarians who survived the decade were still employed in the same place at the same chores.

The disadvantaged minorities that Wiseman treated with such effectiveness continued throughout the decade to be among the most rewarding subjects for broadcast essayists. At networks and local stations alike, the poor, the handicapped, the young, the old, the abused, the sick, the dying, those with a different sexual orientation—all had their gifted chroniclers. Among the dozens of examples viewed this past season, a few were particularly moving, including Bill Moyers's gentle and affectionate "Anyplace but Here," an hour which broke through the insulation that surrounds big-city mental institutions and their unfortunate inmates, and "The Word Is Out," two hours that gave a frequently unheard or misunderstood minority—the openly homosexual community, male and female—its clearest, least prejudicial treatment to date.

"Epitaph for Mom," WHIO-TV Dayton reporter Martha Dunsky's tribute to one woman's life and death, in its low-keyed telling offered universal insights. So did Dorothy Tod's "What If You Couldn't Read?"—the story of how one middle-aged man overcame illiteracy in the Vermont backcountry.

Finally, in Ed Bradley's *CBS Report* on "The Boat People," the decade's recurring preoccupation with the woes of common humanity was given an international focus in a deeply disturbing portrayal of the ongoing effects of that living-room war we would just as soon forget.

1/Politics and Broadcasting: The Odd Couple

Watergate demonstrated just how nasty politicians and broadcasters could be to each other. But if no love was lost, neither was any opportunity for gain overlooked. Nor was this ambivalence limited to the events surrounding Watergate. The reciprocal needs of American politics and American broadcasting increased throughout the decade. And the couple was as much at odds at the end of the 1970s as at the beginning.

Politics dominated the first DuPont-Columbia Survey just as politics had dominated air time in the season of 1968–69. Convention coverage had traditionally been the Olympics of network TV, with the winner assumed to be the industry leader for the succeeding four years. In 1968 for the first time, one network, ABC, drew back from the exigencies of gavel-to-gavel coverage in favor of a nightly package, leaving the two remaining networks to fight it out. Even so, network expenses for the presidential primaries, conventions, campaigns, and election in 1968 totaled more than $30.7 million as compared to $25 million four years before. By 1980, that figure was expected to top $130 million.

When one tuned in the Republicans in Miami in early August 1968, ABC's cutback appeared more than justified. With the conclusion foregone, the proceedings carefully machined to accommodate camera and microphone, the celebrations and suspense equally phony, all the time, effort, and money expended seemed a wicked waste, an elaborate put-on in which broadcasters and politicians connived in equal parts.

The Democratic convention in Chicago, however, was quite another matter. Hampered by an electricians' strike and lack of cooperation by local authorities, the networks found themselves facing the biggest story of the year and one of the biggest challenges in the history of broadcast journalism. As the first Survey reported, events in the convention hall and outside transformed TV newsmen

> from observers, supposedly with professional privileges . . . into participants and finally into active antagonists—challenged not only on the streets and in the parks of Chicago, and on the convention floor, but by a large segment of the viewing public as well. It wasn't that they were considered unfair in their presentation so much as they were held somehow mystically responsible for the violence they reported. Ten weeks later, television's coverage of the street riots and what occurred afterward inside the convention hall was blamed by many Democrats for their defeat at the polls.

This suspicion of television and its part in the outcome of any given event was not limited to Democrats or to the year 1968. It persisted and grew with the decade, reaching a climax in the recriminations that accompanied and followed Watergate. Even after

Nixon and his confreres had departed the scene, television and its "meddling" journalists remained the politicians' favored scapegoat or excuse.

And yet this growing dislike and suspicion in no way inhibited politicians (or anyone else with something to sell) from trying to use the media. A politician's ability to catch the TV camera's attention and hold it was considered critical to success. And if these transactions were not motivated by love—well, then, money could usually turn the trick.

Broadcast expenditures for Nixon's successful 1968 campaign rose to about $12.6 million, versus $6.1 million for Hubert Humphrey. Total radio and TV time charges for all candidates—federal, state, and local—which had reached $34.6 million in 1964, jumped to $58.9 million in 1968. When production costs were added, the estimate went as high as $89 million.

Mid-term elections were no exception. In 1970 the total broadcasting bill had climbed to $50.3 million, from $32 million in the elections of 1966. According to the *Congressional Quarterly*, "the outstanding political upsets of 1970 have been made by men of great wealth presenting their politics to the voters on television and spending their way from obscurity to success in a matter of weeks."

Not everyone agreed it was that simple. According to no less an authority than media consultant Roger Ailes, Nixon's highly successful TV adviser for the 1968 campaign, the results in 1970 were highly ambiguous. Ailes's comment:

> In the thirty-five gubernatorial races of 1970, nineteen winners did indeed outspend their op-

ponents on television and radio, but sixteen men who also outspent the opposition on the broadcasting media lost. In winning in New York, Nelson Rockefeller spent more than three times the amount spent on broadcasting by Arthur Goldberg. In Arkansas, Winthrop Rockefeller outspent Dale Bumpers three to one on broadcasting—and lost, collecting only one third of the total votes.

Media experts like Ailes, who packaged politicians and presented them to the public, particularly on TV, had become notorious—thanks to Joe McGinniss's 1969 best-seller on the Nixon candidacy, *The Selling of the President, 1968.* By 1980 the political consultant was so taken for granted as to become almost invisible.* But retaining these expert services, like hiring news consultants in another sector of broadcasting, guaranteed little more than meeting the competition.

Nonetheless, money continued to speak, and the cash demanded for a successful candidacy (much of it ticketed for TV) continued to discourage the poor but honest aspirant from throwing a hat in the ring or forced him or her to pluck it out midway. The average Senate candidate spent about $920,000 in 1978, as opposed to just under $600,000 in 1976. Eleven Senate candidates spent more than $1 million apiece, and one—Jesse Helms of North Carolina—invested $7.5 million to ensure his reelection. Expenditures for House candidates had climbed from an average of $71,000 to $108,000.

---

*These experts had become exports as well. In 1978, competitors David Garth and Joseph Napolitan took sides in the Venezuelan presidential elections; after a $100 million campaign, Garth's candidate won by a 3.4 percent margin.

The 875 candidates for 470 seats spent $150 million for their primary and general election campaigns. And figures showed that in the 1978 Senate races the bigger spender won out in 85 percent of the cases, in the House in 82 percent.

Of these formidable budgets, 50 percent went to advertising, with much of that earmarked for the broadcast media. Since 1968, the cost of a 30-second spot had more than doubled for most local and network TV. And despite the 1972 enactment of legislation requiring broadcasters to charge candidates their lowest rates, the price tags on political ads reflected the increase. The number of spots required to catch and hold the attention of the public—now under the lash of a killing competition—had increased by about 25 percent, by Roger Ailes's estimate.

Legislation passed to discourage this cash-and-carry approach to political office helped little. Although individual contributors had been limited to $25,000, with a $1,000 lid on any contribution to one candidate's election per year, the money still rolled in. Appeals on television were particularly effective. In 1978, money contributed to congressional candidates by political action committees, formed to get around legislation limiting the contributions of individuals and corporations, amounted to nearly $35.1 million. Four years earlier, contributions to congressional candidates by such committees were only $12.5 million. In 1980, political action committees were expected to make a total of $50 million available to the congressional candidates who seemed most likely to further their particular causes or projects.

There seemed little likelihood of relief from this

climbing spiral.* The fall of 1979 saw the most expensive gubernatorial campaign in history take place in Louisiana where, thanks to rising air charges and a year-long campaign, cumulative costs to the six candidates totaled $20 million.

The calendar was constantly being advanced in presidential politics as well. In 1968, the New Hampshire primaries in March had been established by some inscrutable agreement between politicians and journalists as the first bellwether of things to come at convention time in midsummer. By 1976, the Iowa caucus in January had become a harbinger. And by the 1980 elections the first significant indication of a trend had been more or less arbitrarily assigned to the November straw polls in Florida. However obscure and inconclusive the media acknowledged this last event to be, they covered it massively and the politicians went along, spending substantial sums to sway the inconsequential vote.

The 1980 presidential campaign opened in earnest so far as the networks were concerned on the night before Halloween, 1979, when candidate John Connally paid CBS $28,500 plus $2,500 editing charges for a five-minute prime-time spot produced by the aforementioned Roger Ailes. This broadcast resulted in four thousand calls to the Connally campaign—most of them prospective volunteers whose efforts and donations were spent to try to persuade voters to choose Connally over front-runner Ronald Reagan in a Florida

*Common Cause, though, maintained that since matching federal funds had become available to presidential candidates, there had been a reduction in political action committee contributions to those candidates. (In the meantime, Common Cause was pushing for matching funds for congressional candidates.)

state convention straw poll on November 17. The results: Reagan, 36.4 percent of the vote; Connally, 26.1 percent.

The first real unpleasantness between politicians and broadcasters in the 1980 campaign arose when President Carter asked for the privilege of buying a half hour of prime time in the first week of December 1979 to announce his candidacy, and all three networks turned him down. With a full year to go before the election, CBS was limiting its commercials to the five minutes granted Connally. ABC said they were not accepting political advertising before 1980, and NBC, too, indicated the Carter request was premature, pointing out that the earliest half-hour block sold by a network in the previous presidential campaign had been March 31, 1976. Unwilling to take no for an answer, Carter went to the FCC, which voted four to three in favor of his being given the time.* Despite the President's victory, the crisis in Iran prompted him to cut back his presentation to a brief five minutes that CBS provided on December 4.

The Iran crisis also prompted President Carter to withdraw from a debate, sponsored by the *Des Moines Register and Tribune,* scheduled for January 7. (The

*The networks, however, appealed the Commission's decision in the U.S. Court of Appeals. While the networks said the FCC "has thrust itself too deeply into the political process and assumed an editorial role . . . that violates First Amendment principles" (ABC), the FCC maintained that the networks wanted "to remain the sole arbiter of when, who, and how much the public hears during the presidential campaign." Siding with the FCC was the Carter-Mondale Committee, which along with eleven politically diverse groups and individuals—ranging from the Americans for Democratic Action to James L. Buckley—filed friend-of-the-court briefs. Both sides were still presenting their cases the first week of January.

crisis, however, did not prevent the Carter-Mondale Committee from purchasing a half hour from ABC, on January 6, for an early evening political documentary featuring Carter.) The debate, originally intended to include only Carter and Senator Kennedy, had been opened to Governor Edmund G. Brown, Jr., after he mounted an Iowa campaign. All three networks and PBS had planned coverage of the forum, but the debate was canceled when Carter backed out. The Republican debate—with candidates Connally, Howard Baker, Robert Dole, Philip Crane, John Anderson, and George Bush—was carried live only by PBS.

Although the networks protested that each year the political campaigns began earlier and cost them more, there was no indication of their soft-peddling political items in their day-to-day coverage.

This precession of the campaigns under the influence of TV newsmen was just one further demonstration of a phenomenon disturbing to many: The press, particularly its electronic elements, not only was dictating the behavior of the candidates but in the opinion of many was usurping the power of political bosses and machines.

One means, of course, was the proliferation of surveys and polls, from the earliest reaches of the campaign to election night. Frequently initiated by broadcasters, and reported and interpreted on the air, these studies often became the uncritically accepted milestones in a politician's climb or descent.

However astronomical the increase in expenses, however persistent the attention paid by TV and radio news to political matters, the fact remained—and it was a disquieting one—that the percentage of Americans exercising their franchise diminished year after year. If candidate expenditures were considered an effort to buy the vote, the cost per ballot had skyrocketed in the last ten years.

In November 1978, the percentage of turnout—37.9 percent of those eligible—was the lowest since wartime 1942 and off over ten percentage points from a peak of 48.1 percent in 1962. According to the Committee for the Study of the American Electorate, the reasons were

> the decay of political and social institutions, most notably the political party; the growing impotence felt by the citizen in the face of large public and private institutions and increasingly complex problems; the role that mass media, especially television, has in creating confusion in the minds of some.

The nation's apparent declining interest in politics —even while it was handing over offices more and more frequently to the electronically adaptable and well-heeled—found clear expression on election evening November 7, 1978. Prime-time coverage by the three networks of that day's off-year election commanded only 44 percent of the total TV audience, the first election night when the number of people tuned in dropped below a simple majority. In 1974, 57 percent of the TV sets on had been tuned to the network affiliates during the comparable period, and in 1970 the networks had commanded 71 percent of the audience for their election-evening coverage. In 1978, independent stations on both coasts were demolishing their network affiliates with movies like *The Pink Panther, The Graduate, Bonnie and Clyde,* and *The Great Waldo Pepper.*

If massive television coverage had a negative effect

in discouraging people from going to the polls, its impact on political careers could be devastating. From the disastrous Democratic convention of 1968 through Watergate and the Ford-Carter debates of 1976, right up to Roger Mudd's on-air disentombment of Chappaquiddick in the fall of 1979, the critical contribution of the media was acknowledged even when it was deplored. In an increasing number of contests, the assumptions and incantations of reporters took precedence over whatever issues the cowed politicians cared, or dared, to articulate. Themes were developed and orchestrated by the press, and even when it was to their drastic disadvantage the principals seemed hypnotically to sing along.

In the campaign of 1972, the stampede of press coverage following the exposure of Thomas Eagleton's unfortunate history of mental illness and McGovern's uncertain response showed this journalistic-political phenomenon at its worst. The whole course of the Carter-Ford campaign, with Jimmy's "lust in the heart" vying with Jerry's unfortunate lapse concerning Poland, ran counter to any serious exposure of the candidates' attitudes on substantive issues. This situation was eloquently described on the *ABC Evening News* by Howard K. Smith:

> The campaign has been, in a word, banal. . . . The public has the feeling of being nibbled to death by ducks, not addressed by titans as should be the case in a contest to choose not only our President, but the *ex officio* leader of a troubled Western civilization. The men have but thirty days to dissolve the impression visibly growing but which we all dread to accept: neither has the stature for the job.

Smith didn't pursue the point that a TV screen, such as the one he was appearing on, could be an enormously effective stature-reducer.

These phenomena could perhaps have been more easily tolerated if another trend hadn't become apparent as the decade proceeded: The same abject attitudes assumed by politicians in pursuit of office seemed to carry over even after victory was won. Politicians, once in office, continued to bow to the tyranny of the media and the polls.

It was a far cry from the days of the imperial presidency, when Nixon, in an eight-month period, went on the tube five times during the prime evening hours to recommend his policies in Vietnam to the American public. Senator William Fulbright had reacted in alarm:

> Unfortunately, Congress is at a great disadvantage in the war powers debate, as it is in discussing most issues, because the Executive has a near monopoly on effective access to the public attention. The President can command a national television audience to hear his views on controversial matters at prime time—on short notice, at whatever length he chooses, and at no expense to the federal government or to his party. Other constitutional office-holders are compelled to rely on highly selective newspaper articles and television news spots, which at most will convey bits and snatches of their points of view, usually selected in such a way as to create an impression of cranky carping at an heroic and beleaguered President. . . .
>
> The only reliable way of getting the media to swallow an idea is by candy-coating it with a prediction or accusation. . . . Communication is power, and exclusive access to it is a dangerous unchecked power. Television has done as much to expose the

powers of the President as would a constitutional amendment formally abolishing the co-equality of the three branches of government.

Senator Harold Hughes of Iowa agreed:

> The system of checks and balances is, in point of fact, checkmated, unless the legislature is afforded equivalent opportunity to present its point of view to the American people. In these times, there could be no more potent influence working toward centralization of power in the executive branch and the dilution of the constitutional prerogatives of the legislative branch than such an imbalance in access to the mass media.

The legislative branch more than got its own back in the Watergate hearings and the impeachment proceedings that followed. And a decade later, the legislative branch of Congress seemed very much to be calling the scattershots.

Not that Jimmy Carter hadn't started out apparently on top of the tube. Nixon took one approach: He faced hostility but knew better than any previous president how to make the media work for him—only to see all his cleverness finally boomerang. Carter began in a different way, emphasizing honesty, directness, and an open presidency to generally benign—even indifferent—media. Carter began his term as "the most readily available president in recent history," with regularly scheduled fortnightly press conferences, supplemented by fireside chats, radio call-ins, and town meetings.* In three months, his popularity in the polls had

---

*Another Carter accommodation inaugurated in December 1978 included 30- to 90-second actualities of administration officials' speeches. The free service was made available to broadcasters

risen twelve points above where it stood at his inauguration.

By June 1979, thanks to a combination of inflation and the energy situation, Carter's popularity had dropped more drastically than in any recent presidency except Nixon's, and the open presidency had to all intents and purposes long since disappeared.* On July 1, 1978, Carter summoned back Gerald Rafshoon, the public relations expert who had packaged his successful 1976 campaign, as full-time media consultant. Almost immediately thereafter, public relations expediency was given credit for crucial White House decisions.

James Wooten, in *Esquire*, wrote that Rafshoon

> concerned himself with everything from policy to politics, from cosmetics to rhetoric, from immediate objectives to long-range goals . . . dictating style and participating in substance, urging the President to veto a defense authorization bill, prodding him to continue slashing funds from western water projects. . . . Rafshoon is always there—on taxes, on Israel and Egypt, on China and Taiwan, on Iran, on guns versus butter, on inflation versus recession. . . . In essence, Rafshoon has assumed control of every aspect of the President's public contacts.

Even more pointed were the comments of adman Jack Geller in *Television/Radio Age:*

---

around the nation who dialed a toll-free phone number in Washington for the recorded clips. By December 1979 the service was registering four hundred calls a day.

*But as a result of the Iran crisis in November–December 1979, Carter's popularity climbed back steeply from 32 to 61 percent in a single month.

Here is a man who was *not* elected by the American people or confirmed by the United States Senate for any office. He has little or no experience in domestic or foreign affairs. Yet he appears to have more power than any member of the Cabinet . . . the only reason this man is permitted to participate in the formulation of presidential decisions is that he is the advertising agency executive, specializing in television, who helped Candidate Carter become President Carter. . . . I suggest that he return to Atlanta and start to prepare media plans for his client's 1980 campaign. If he wants to be involved in making governmental decisions, let him run for public office and wait until he is elected.

Although Rafshoon ostensibly was there to improve Carter's relations with the press as well as his public image, things became so bad that in July 1979 Carter shut down his fortnightly press conferences. As with other presidents before him, Carter's dissatisfaction with the press centered in Washington. In reply to a question from Daniel Schorr about his relations with the White House press corps, Carter replied, "I think it's better for me not to have all the questions focused on me by a group that's almost exclusively oriented within Washington. . . . I would like to let my voice be heard and felt, and the questions be heard by me and felt, from various places in the country."

After hostile press coverage of his peremptory cabinet dismissals in the summer of 1979—criticism that Carter termed "grossly distorted" and "exaggerated"— he announced his intention of bypassing the Washington news corps and going directly to the grass roots. ABC's White House correspondent Sam Donaldson said of Carter and his advisers, "They're angry. We're their enemies.... It is a circle-the-wagons mentality."* NBC's Judy Woodruff added, "Jody [Powell] carries a huge grudge against the press. It's not new."

George Reedy, former press secretary for Lyndon Johnson and now professor of journalism at Marquette University, said Carter's attempt to bypass the Washington press corps was bound to fail. He wrote in *The New York Times:*

> The President's image is made by the impact of what he does—not by the press's words in describing it. Folksy stories extolling presidential goodness will not soothe the anger of motorists in gas lines. The White House press secretary can "create images" without obtaining the support of the housewife who discovers that milk has gone up another four cents a half gallon. A trip to a New England town meeting will not be regarded by an auto worker as adequate compensation for loss of a job. Presidents rise or fall on the basis of performance; rhetoric, no matter how well stage-managed, is secondary.
>
> These points are not so apparent in the White House—partly because it *is* possible through intelligently directed public relations techniques to produce "favorable" stories. This is especially true of Mr. Carter, who obviously impresses small groups as an honest, sincere man who wants to do

*Donaldson retaliated by filing a story of a town meeting in which President Carter was asked by a woman whether he had caught any fish and Carter went out of his way to thank the lady and point out, "That's the kind of question I'd never get from the Washington press corps." Elsewhere Carter complained that the press's concerns were "just frivolous, little superficial transient questions that come up in cocktail parties here in Washington."

the right thing. When journalists write such stories, however, they create another problem: The public sees the whole thing as a P.R. campaign to "manipulate" the press; and the total effect is negative. . . . The people do want to feel that the president is speaking to them simply and directly. A P.R. campaign gives the opposite impression. . . . Mr. Carter will discover that there are no shortcuts. If things are going reasonably well in 1980, he will be renominated and reelected despite press enmity; if poorly, he will be defeated regardless of press sympathy.

However wise and well-informed Reedy's observation, he was offering advice that assumed a forbearance on the part of broadcasters and an openness on the part of politicians that neither was as yet ready to risk.

2/The Impossible Necessity

In 1969, the initial Alfred I. duPont-Columbia Survey reported the creation of the first one-hour daily network news program, accomplished by doubling the time allotment of the *Joe Benti News Show* and renaming it the *CBS Morning News*. On the eve of this not inconsiderable event in the history of television news, Richard Salant, president of CBS News and the man responsible for increasing the evening news from fifteen to thirty minutes just six years earlier, stated, "We need an hour news show every night. . . . We can't give stories enough length or depth. Things are always left out."

Ten years later, in 1979, the *CBS Morning News* was still the only one-hour daily network news program on the air, and however fine its performance record, it enjoyed the least support from affiliates, sponsors, and viewers. Salant, being retired against his will after sixteen years of service as the most powerful and effective news executive in the nation, was still saying, "It's going to come some day. Not before April 30."

Bill Leonard, upon his elevation to the CBS News

presidency as Salant's successor, said about expanding the evening news, "There's a tiny light at the end of the tunnel. It may not happen on my shift [Leonard at age sixty-three had less than two full years of service ahead of him], but sure as hell we'll see it."

For ten years, broadcast newspeople had been begging for more time to do what radio and TV admittedly did best: the news. CBS's most popular employee, Walter Cronkite, had put it eloquently at the 1976 national meeting of the Radio and Television News Directors Association when he warned his fellow journalists, "We fall far short of presenting all, or even a goodly part, of the news each day that a citizen would need to intelligently exercise his franchise in this democracy. So as he *depends* more and more on us, presumably the depth of knowledge of the average man diminishes. This clearly can lead to disaster in a democracy."

Two years before that, addressing the same group, Elmer Lower, departing the top news job at ABC, had said, "We've already taken some surveys and studies regarding the practicality and potential of a full hour of news on the network. Personally, I know it's possible, and I think it's not only desirable, but practical. My own prediction is that an hour news program on some network in the evening will be a fact of viewing life in the not too distant future. Five years at the most, more likely earlier."

Actually, the very year when Cronkite saw the republic threatened by its skimpy allotment of TV news, all three networks had solemnly declared their intention of doing what he and his fellow broadcast journalists recommended. Said CBS President Arthur Taylor, making his lofty pitch to network affiliates at their annual meeting in May 1976, "We do part of the job today —although it has been said, with perhaps some truth, that we provide not much more than a good headline service.

"Why should we have a goal of providing more? Not for us. Not even for you. But for the man, the woman, who must know more if he is to live more."

A matter of life and death to the Republic, to its citizens—but the CBS affiliates were not moved. No more were the affiliates at NBC and ABC. In a few months the idea put so firmly forward by all three networks was declared unworkable and abandoned. The avowed reason on the part of affiliates was their unwillingness to reduce their local news service and relinquish another half hour to the already dominant networks. The networks' excuse: a reluctance to cross the affiliates.* The excuses on both sides lacked substance, according to *TV Guide:*

> We really couldn't care less whether the stations or the networks profit from expanded network news. We do know that if television is to serve in "the public interest, convenience, and necessity," which is what the Communications Act demands, network news must be expanded.
>
> We respectfully request that stations and networks get off dead center, find a way to split the

---

*One important factor standing in the way of network news expansion had been the arrival in 1971 of the FCC's prime-time access rule which in effect returned a half hour at the beginning of the evening to network affiliates in the top fifty markets. Intended like so many federal regulations to improve service to the public, in this instance to encourage important local programming, it had instead opened another half hour to mindless game shows and situation comedies. It also effectively prevented the networks from expanding their newscasts into the adjacent half hour.

loot equitably, and pay more attention to the public.

Actually, the matter was far from closed. If Salant seemed wistful on the subject as he prepared to depart from CBS, later, when he startled the industry by announcing his new job as vice-chairman of NBC, the sixty-minute news format was prominent on his agenda. "It's an idea whose time has come," he reaffirmed. "People just haven't recognized it yet." Salant was thinking not of taking back a half hour from the affiliates but of returning to them the 7:00 to 7:30 network news slot and putting his expanded network news in the peak prime-time hour of 8:00 to 9:00 P.M.*

Speaking to the editors of *The New York Times* the week before he took his new job, Salant explained his thinking. "How could they [the affiliates] complain when they'd be getting back 365 half hours a year to use in their own way?" Salant also claimed he could save the network millions of dollars in programming costs. To add thirty minutes to the existing evening news would, by his reckoning, cost a mere $5,000 a night, compared to $250,000 an episode for a typical half-hour prime-time entertainment show.

There were other reasons for the sixty-minute evening news. "The networks are running out of material on the entertainment side. They're repeating themselves and reaching to extremes to come up with new program concepts. But in the news, there's something new every day.

---

*This idea had already been put forward by former Group W president Don McGannon—the man responsible for the prime-time access rule and an outspoken advocate of those two apparently irreconcilable desiderata: quality programming and affiliates' rights.

"I've always felt you have a tougher time with news on a leading network because the air time is so much more valuable that they hate to give it up. NBC is not doing so well today, and therefore may be more likely to try something as radical as this."* Finally, "As a policymaker myself at NBC . . . I'll be able to make the argument among peers. At CBS, the news division is so insulated that we didn't always have access to top management."

Although one of the recurring nightmares of network news operations had been lack of insulation and the possibility of intrusion from top management, there was no question that Salant in his new and elevated managerial spot represented the best and brightest hope to date for the sixty-minute network newscast.

Two months before Salant came on board, NBC president Fred Silverman had said, "I don't believe we're any closer to an hour news. There are major problems, and they're justifiable problems with the affiliates at all three networks. The only way we could do an hour news would be to cut back the local news, and I would have to agree with them that is a disservice to the local communities."

The month after Salant's arrival, Silverman was saying to the affiliates, "Maybe we'll all decide an extra half hour of prime-time news is more important than an existing half hour of entertainment." He added that he was "figuring out a way for us to expand *Nightly News* without reducing your service."

---

*Actually, regular prime-time news was already a reality on all three networks with the so-called news breaks and news briefs (staccato one-minute recaps of the evening news stuck between programs) commanding the highest ratings and prices of any news on the air.

Although reports had it that Silverman was waiting until NBC became "preeminent" in the news, which meant beating Salant's old team at CBS and holding off the encroachments of ABC, it still sounded as if Salant had found a more receptive ear than he had had to date.

Meanwhile, the primary scandal of American journalism remained that as TV news had grown to be the main source of news for a substantial majority of the nation, and the only news source for at least a third of all America, there had been, despite the overwhelming increase in profits and circulation, no commensurate increase in regularly delivered service. The news departments at the three networks, no matter how great their expertise and knowledge, were still trying—as their foremost anchorman, Walter Cronkite, so tellingly put it—"to fit one hundred pounds of news into the one-pound sack that we are given to fill each night."

In addition to the sixty-minute nightly news, Salant had another plan as exciting and difficult to attain: the establishment of a regular weekly period in the prime-time schedule for full-length news documentaries. The last year a network could lay claim to such a luxury was 1969, when Salant himself presided over the dismantling of the old *CBS Reports* weekly hour in order to give alternate weeks to the struggling young magazine *60 Minutes.* What had happened to news documentaries since was described by Salant himself some ten years later:

> They hide them. They put them in the places where they'll do the least damage. You wait to see where the competition is going to run the Oscars and you put them in there. If [only] you had regu-

larity, so people will know they're coming, once a week, and it's a habit, and you know sufficiently in advance so you can publicize them, advertise them. Sometimes we're not even told in time for us to get a listing.*

At the beginning of the decade, network documentarians could look back with some sense of immediacy to the golden days of Ed Murrow and Fred Friendly— of *See It Now, CBS Reports,* and the *NBC White Papers.* As the 1970s drew to a close, whatever their individual triumphs, ten more years of indifference and neglect by network management, sponsors, and the public stood between them and the good old days.

As far back as 1969, the DuPont-Columbia Survey had reported that of the thirty top TV spenders (representing total advertising budgets of $1.3 billion), none had chosen to bankroll a network news documentary that season. The record over the decade was not to improve; neither did public attention to documentaries increase. If anything, documentary ratings were lower than ever. James Rosenfield, president of the CBS Television Network, told the New England chapter of the National Academy of Television Arts and Sciences in October 1978 that although the network documentary units were tops so far as artistry was concerned and dealt with "the major issues of our times," they suffered what could only be described as "massive rejection" by the public. As proof he cited Nielsen reports which showed that, of six recent CBS documentaries, five

*Two prototypes for regular prime-time news documentary shows were announced before Salant's departure from CBS: one on investigative reporting of the recent past, hosted by Mike Wallace, another a science series with Walter Cronkite. Each appeared once during the summer of 1979.

finished last in the weekly ratings and one next to last. His conclusion: "Are we going to go on doing documentaries? Of course we are, in spite of a discouraging vote like this. Because you can't have a fully rounded news service without them—and a full service is part of the mandate of CBS News. But it's not for business reasons and, God knows, it's not for ratings reasons."

Still, the networks in the season of 1978–79 could only be described as grudging in their allotment of prime time to their documentary units. Gene Jankowski, president of the CBS Broadcasting Group, promised twenty hours of prime-time documentaries for the 1979–80 season, the same number offered in the previous twelve months. By December, five hours had been aired.

NBC, which had ten and a half hours of prime-time documentaries to its credit in 1978–79, pointed with pride to the revival of the *NBC White Paper* defunct since 1974, to be sponsored in 1979–80 by the Weyerhaeuser paper company. By midseason only one White Paper had been aired and one more was scheduled. Otherwise, the score for prime-time documentaries at NBC by December 1979 stood at five hours. And ABC, whose ten *Closeups* represented the most consistently hard-hitting prime-time documentaries of the 1978–79 season, had delivered two by December, with ten more scheduled for the 1979–80 season.

If NBC's documentary record had yet to reflect the presence of its potent new partisan, Salant had other promises to fulfill: namely, the spreading of news throughout the program schedule, as it occurred, "because of the reliance the public has on us." This gave hope of at least one network's return to live coverage of events local, national, and international, which was one of the glories of television in the long-ago days of the McCarthy, McClellan, and Kefauver hearings and the early Security Council sessions at the United Nations. For starters, NBC was projecting live coverage of the enormously important SALT II debates in the Senate scheduled for fall 1979. That they were not seen before 1980 was not the network's fault.

Meanwhile, the news departments of NBC, CBS, and ABC were continuing to let others do the important and fascinating business of covering the world live. The Panama Canal debates in 1978 got no live coverage from the networks, although National Public Radio carried the full 300 hours. Network live coverage of Pope John Paul II's visit to the United States totaled 9½ hours on NBC, 4¾ hours on CBS, and 6½ hours on ABC— none of this in prime time. When John Paul II ran opposite pro football, pro football naturally won out. The only television operation that stuck with the Pope throughout his trip was the Spanish International Network, with seventeen TV affiliates and three hundred subscribing cable outlets, which racked up a total of 47½ hours of live coverage.

Fidel Castro, who made his first visit to the United Nations in nineteen years on October 12, 1979, got no live coverage on the commercial networks, although PBS carried his ninety-minute speech in its entirety. And the commercial networks were not present for such important UN events as Cambodian Prime Minister Norodom Sihanouk's appearance before the Security Council in January 1979 or the Security Council Palestinian rights debates in August 1979. Even the Iran crisis did nothing to attract the commercial networks' attention to the United Nations, although

WNET fed PBS seven hours live from the Security Council.

Such obvious live-TV fare as the opening of the Kennedy Library in Boston in October 1979, which offered President Carter back to back with his primary Democratic challenger, Ted Kennedy, as well as the political debut of a brand-new generation of America's premier political dynasty in the maiden speech of Joe Kennedy III, was ignored by all TV networks. And of the 922 hours of continuous coverage of the House of Representatives made available for the first time in March 1979, the commercial networks had still carried none live by Christmas time of that year.

The fate of the excellent special reports on current major news events, which all three networks produced on a regular basis, was discouraging. Of the 137 such specials produced by the three networks combined between July 1, 1978, and June 30, 1979, thirty-five, or less than one per month per network, were offered the maximum prime-time audiences they deserved. ABC's nightly series of quarter- and half-hour sum-ups of the riveting crisis in Iran, however admirable and important, had to give pride of place to its somewhat less admirable prime-time schedule.

If most of Richard Salant's efforts to improve and expand broadcast journalism's position in the past decade had been defeated or deflected, and if his favorable impact on his new network had yet to register on the air, he could nevertheless point to several major accomplishments.

First and foremost was *60 Minutes,* the only network news program in history to find a regular place in the weekly Nielsen top ten ratings. But *60 Minutes* hadn't won its first place on the rating charts quickly or easily. The record-setting magazine show began in September 1968 by alternating Tuesday evenings with *CBS Reports.* In those days, the program was required once a month to give up half its time to local affiliates.

In the fall of 1971 the struggling magazine show was removed from prime time and given an hour in the late Sunday afternoon ghetto, where for half its season it was subject to sudden and summary preemption by professional football. It stayed in this slot for four seasons, except for the summer months, when it was bounced around the prime-time schedule. During this uncertain time, thinly viewed and sponsored, the show was regularly threatened with extinction by network programmers.

In 1975, instead of being eliminated outright, *60 Minutes* was pushed forward to buck NBC's *Wonderful World of Disney.* Miraculously, *60 Minutes,* with its solid diet of investigative journalism and expert features, not only survived but thrived, and by 1976 it was guaranteed its full hour no matter how long the football game went on. In 1978 it ranked in the top ten twenty-three times. But there was no plan to eliminate the summer reruns that had depressed its ratings off-season.

CBS's *60 Minutes* had won out, whether its history was seen as heartening proof of network persistence and audience intelligence and loyalty or as a depressing example of just how difficult it was for quality nonfiction programming to break through the resistance of commercial network honchos and uptight sponsors to catch the attention of a dull, apathetic audience.

Not only had it won out, it had earned that final

accolade of media success: an army of imitators.* Among these were such tries as CBS's short-lived *Who's Who* and *People* and NBC's *Prime Time Sunday,* which had gained the dubious distinction early in its run of being watched by fewer people than any other regularly scheduled prime-time network series. At midseason *Prime Time Sunday* was changed to *Prime Time Saturday* in hopes of increasing its audience.

After a shaky start, ABC's *20/20* was more successful, managing to make its way into the top ten two times between June and December 1979.

Success in no way spoiled the journalistic style and enterprise of *60 Minutes.* To Mike Wallace, executive producer Don Hewitt had added Morley Safer and Dan Rather, two of the network's best reporters, veterans of Vietnam and Washington in the Watergate years, and invited Harry Reasoner to return to his original assignment after an eight-year absence at ABC. Although purists sometimes took exception to the choice of subjects and the means—sometimes approaching entrapment—used to extract stories from reluctant interviewees, *60 Minutes* maintained an impressive record for combining audience appeal with expert journalism.

The most serious criticism that could be launched against *60 Minutes* was one that really was not its fault. Its success and the rush to imitate it seemed to diminish

---

*Other early magazine shows less fortunate than *60 Minutes* included NET's *Public Broadcasting Laboratory,* the prototype of most TV magazines, and NBC's *First Tuesday,* which was slotted against *60 Minutes* for two impressive seasons. Still hanging on was CBS's admirable daytime *Magazine,* which had been appearing at irregular times and intervals since 1974 and had not yet been able to commandeer a regular weekly position in the stream of game shows and soap operas that had been the daytime offerings of broadcasters since the heyday of network radio.

the likelihood of any of the three networks' finding prime time for the regular airing of hour-long documentaries—first because the magazine format was being given priority and second because subjects worthy of extended treatment were appropriated for briefer magazine-length attention. Indeed, confronted by the success of *60 Minutes,* the most prestigious documentary series in the business, *CBS Reports,* for a while was dividing its precious hour into three segments— one reason Bill Moyers mentioned for giving up commercial TV and returning to public broadcasting. CBS Group President Gene Jankowski put it this way: "The big challenge of the networks is to package information that the public ought to have in ways that would make them want to watch it."*

Salant's parting legacy—and a handsome one it was —was the new CBS News *Sunday Morning* program, a weekly news anthology produced by one of TV's top documentary talents, Robert (Shad) Northshield. With a staff of seasoned professionals and a generous hour and a half at its disposal, it could take on major stories as well as pursuing the off-beat, without seeming to squander time needed for more substantial items. The result, presided over by a relaxed and literate Charles Kuralt, was another demonstration of how well a network news operation could use the time given to it.

But even here the blessing was mixed. Fine though *Sunday Morning* was, the fact remained that rather than displacing any of the worthless fare that cluttered

*At the other extreme from the magazine's shorter takes was the jumbo whole-evening package, which had been tried with indifferent success, including CBS's three hours on energy and NBC's three hours on the American family.

the airwaves day in and day out, it forced off the air *Camera Three,* a fixture since 1956. Like such former network offerings as Cousteau and the National Geographic, not to mention most top-quality drama and music, the venerable series found refuge on the Public Broadcasting Service, prompting a repetition of the query, How much of its better self could commercial TV relinquish and still survive?

3/The Advent of ABC

In 1968, when the DuPont-Columbia Survey began its observations, there were essentially two major daily network news shows fighting it out in the early evening. CBS and NBC had been trying for first place since the half-hour news came into existence. With a limited budget, a small staff, and only 124 affiliates subscribing to its newscast, ABC was a noncompeting third.

Ten years later, ABC had drawn up alongside the leaders not only in money spent and personnel hired but in quality of offerings. The network that had taken the lead in ratings and sales of prime-time programming was determined to do the same in news, a confirmation of a relatively new broadcast philosophy articulated by ABC Chairman Leonard Goldenson: "ABC will never be the number one network until we're number one in news."

ABC's strategy for winning had at first seemed to confirm the journalistic purists' worst fears—that the network with the tradition of beating the entertainment competition by programming down as far as the public would tolerate would attempt the same highly successful technique with news. The early indications of change were fairly drastic, including a major capital spending program on electronic news-gathering equipment and a 25 percent increase in staff and budget.

Most sensational of all was the spiriting away of NBC *Today* star Barbara Walters with a $5 million contract. The elevation of Walters, an expert interviewer and popular magazine-cover subject, to the most-valuable-player spot in network news was seen by some as a long overdue demonstration that newswomen were just as worthy of high pay and corporate approval as newsmen. To others it represented a grave insult to the shaky prestige of electronic journalism.

Charles B. Seib, ombudsman for the *Washington Post*, wrote, "We might as well face it. The line between the news business and show business has been erased forever."

Less dramatic, Sander Vanocur, a veteran of the news wars at NBC and PBS who would soon follow Walters to ABC as Washington correspondent, said, "Walters has not done anything to television journalism that it had not already done to itself."

And Walter Cronkite, TV news kingpin who had ostensibly been outclassed, at least so far as pay was concerned, said with characteristic forbearance, insight, and humor, "The Barbara Walters news did shake me up at first, as it did us all. There was a first wave of nausea, the sickening sensation that we were going under, that all of our efforts to hold network television news aloof from show business had failed. But after sleeping on the matter, with more sober, less hysterical reflection, I came to a far less gloomy view." Cronkite chose to find in Walters's jumbo paycheck an acknowledgment by management of the skill and stamina required of top TV newspeople, including himself.

There were further rumblings in January 1977, when the ABC news division was put under the wing of Fred Pierce, president of ABC-TV, another step—industry observers assumed—on the road to converting ABC's news business to show business. Next came the elevation of Roone Arledge, ABC's highly successful head of sports, to the network news presidency. Arledge had a reputation for risk-taking innovation but no journalistic experience behind him. "We had twenty-five years of being noncompetitive to overcome," Arledge said. "We were never even in contention. When I came to the news department we were . . . twelve points behind CBS and eight or nine behind NBC."

Arledge moved Walters from her position as co-anchor with Harry Reasoner to a less conspicuous spot as chief network interviewer and troubleshooter—not, however, before Reasoner announced his intention to return to CBS.

By the summer of 1979, ABC finally reached affiliate parity with CBS and NBC. Not only had circulation and ratings gone up, the quality of the product presented had notably improved. ABC was gaining a reputation for getting there first, looking harder, and staying longer at breaking news events. It aired special reports on Iran every night, beginning November 14, compared to NBC's and CBS's once or twice a week. ABC's two-week sequence on the armaments race, "Second to None?" (two and a half months in the making and totaling fifty-seven minutes on the air), was probably the single most important and effective series mounted by any of the three network newscasts during the season. Here was a reaffirmation of the validity of paying extended attention to important subjects—and by no accident it coincided with the arrival of Stanhope Gould, formerly of NBC and CBS, as a producer for ABC's *World News Tonight.* Gould had scored with a two-part report on Watergate in the fall of 1972 and with his series on the Russian wheat deal the same season.

Segment Three, NBC's impressive series dedicated to the proposition that news should be explored in depth and presented at a decent length, was another expression of this wholesome impulse. Unfortunately, this worthy attempt was deprived of its regular time allotment in the fall of 1979.

From an object of condescension, if not contempt, ABC news by the end of the decade was earning grudging credit and sometimes even admiration. Such marginal operations as its *Good Morning, America,* which married news to show business in the frankest possible way and made spectacular inroads on NBC's long-term front-runner, the *Today* show, added little to the luster of ABC's reputation. Balancing the morning lapses, however, was the most consistently interesting and substantial documentary series on the commercial evening air—the ABC *Closeups,* which included such outstanding achievements during the season as "Arson: Fire for Hire," "The Killing Ground" (on the dumping of poisonous chemical wastes), "Asbestos: The Way to Dusty Death," and "The Shooting of Big Man" (two hours devoted to a single criminal case).

ABC's climbing news ratings (which topped NBC for the first time in April 1979 and hovered in its immediate vicinity thereafter) could be attributed in large part to the growing list of top affiliates that the former "third network" had signed up in recent seasons. But its success in attracting those affiliates had been attributed, among other reasons, to its growing respectability in the news. Most of its new news viewers, ABC claimed, were people who hadn't watched any newscast regularly before.

"I don't think there's any question that we've created a heightened consciousness of news," Marvin Mord, ABC vice-president of research, told *The New York Times'* Les Brown. "We made a decision, when Roone Arledge became president of the news division, that if we were going to make inroads, we'd have to establish a news presence during the entire day. We started doing more news, more news specials, and live coverage of important events. And as the leader in prime time, we were able to do a good job of promoting ABC News and getting new people to try us."

The unfolding story of ABC News, instead of proving the frivolity of the American public and the greed and lack of conscience of network management, suggested that there can, indeed, be a salutory relationship between quality and profits in broadcast journalism.

4/The Local News Scene

Taking the long view, the same happy outcome might be hoped for in the even wilder and woolier news competition that prevailed in local markets from coast to coast. In 1972, local news was reported as outrating network news in eight out of ten of the top TV markets. But if journalistic respectability had maintained the upper hand in network news throughout the decade, this had not always been the case with the local variety.

In a business where a rating point in news could mean hundreds of thousands of dollars in additional station income, television developed its own equivalent to print journalism's circulation wars of the late nineteenth and early twentieth centuries. Presiding over what in many communities deteriorated into an unedifying free-for-all were a new breed of coach-referees called "news consultants."

News consultants were given credit for a variety of eccentric antijournalistic developments that characterized local news operations by mid-decade. These included matching blazers and haircuts, fancy sets, and shorter and softer news items. Anchor people of both sexes were more conspicuous for the brightness of their smiles and the clarity of their skin than for similar qualities in their journalistic prose. There were such developments as the "happy talk" news, which filled the Chicago evenings with cackles and guffaws, and the "kickers, guts, orgasm" approach, which made KGO-TV (ABC's owned-and-operated station in San Francisco) top dog in that wildly competitive market.

Asked to comment on the current status of broadcast journalism, an executive at one of CBS's owned-and-operated stations responded:

> It stinks. Because broadcast stations aren't in the business of news but are in the business of entertainment, there is a serious lack of commitment to news. There's no emphasis on hiring qualified reporters as opposed to pretty faces or mellow voices. News departments are acutely understaffed, and the priorities of most stations are anywhere but on the news department.
>
> Time limitations naturally lead to superficial coverage, and most stations will not make additional time available to go into a topic in depth. When the time is allotted, usually only to fill an FCC requirement, it's often Sunday night or very early in the morning. Some stations which do allot time exercise no judgment in terms of community priorities in what they do cover.

Where once there was simply the evening news, now there was "Newsscene," "The World Tonight," "Eyewitness News," "News Beat," "News Watch." At the height of the San Francisco news wars, reporters were required to don dog masks and cowboy costumes and pose for full-page ads in the local papers.

Under the influence of the consultants, news budgets

rose, along with the heavy-breathing intrusions of management. The average length of a news director's tenure fell to two and a half years, and in many markets reporting staffs turned over even more rapidly. Early in the seventies, one beleaguered West Coast newsman wrote the Survey:

> In the past year, I've spoken with several news directors who are seriously considering other fields of endeavor. . . . There aren't many major markets left where stations don't retain an outside media research and/or consulting service . . . which will screen your shows, critique them, tell you what you're doing wrong, suggest special features to include, etc., etc. Before too many good newsmen leave us, our managers and owners must come to grips with this very real problem. . . . Otherwise, what television news in the future will be is something none of us in the business will recognize . . . an entertaining half-hour or hour with very little of import or significance within it.

Five years later, things had settled down somewhat. Although there was no major local TV news operation that didn't bear the marks of the news consultant invasion, the visibility of these kibitzers had diminished, in part because they were everywhere. Or, if one accepted the comment of an upstate New York news director, recently retired, "The plague of the consultant has come and gone. They have been replaced by a generation of their clones who masquerade as news directors."

Either way, by the end of the decade TV news directors rated consultants tenth in a list of more than twenty possible hazards to quality broadcast journalism. Seen as greater threats were lack of First Amendment protection, the Supreme Court, public apathy, inadequate news budgets and staffs, biased journalism, management greed, too much government regulation, cable, the FCC, and absentee ownership.

If local news was acknowledged as the most important as well as the most lucrative service an individual station could render to its community, quality local news, thanks in part to the influence of the consultants, remained the exception rather than the rule. DuPont Survey correspondents reporting this year on their local stations found the stations' performance questionable. In covering local government, they rated only a quarter of the local stations effective. Coverage of education, women, health, and minorities was rated effective at one out of eight stations, with energy, politics, and community issues doing somewhat better. Coverage of local disasters was highest of all, with one in three stations rated effective.

Correspondent descriptions of the local news scenes, even in those instances where the community boasted one or two outstanding news operations, were frequently mixed and often openly disparaging.

> The most apparent changes in local TV news are cosmetic. Stations are building larger sets and putting more people on them at all times. Also, most stations are obviously attempting to acquire a younger look. Only KSL-TV has kept its anchor people who have been with the station more than 15 years, but it has supplemented them with several co-anchors under the age of 30. The other two stations have replaced all their mature anchor people with young, under 30, fresh-faced, attractive anchors and reporters.
>
> *Salt Lake City, Utah*

In Indiana, we've survived the "happy-talk" consultant era . . . and the formats have softened somewhat. . . . I've a feeling the stations are taking the news more seriously, and that the overall quality of the reporting has improved. Women are, of course, now very visible on the air, and are given regular reporting assignments along with the male reporters. All of the women are very young and, thus, sometimes not as believable as they could be . . . but then most of the men are also very young. All look more or less well turned out and business-like. The women seem to have somewhat more character than the men—there is, I believe, someplace in the world where they turn out men from some kind of a cloning system. . . . They are handsome, speak directly at you, but don't seem to have anything behind those glittering eyes. So perhaps there is a hold-over effect from the consultants' cosmetic conniptions, but only regarding the men. Hair style is less a factor for the men, but still a big problem for the women.

Bloomington, Indiana

[We've seen] the apparently final victory of the news consultants, whose advice is now being followed even by those stations which don't retain them. However, there's an apparent change in the tenor of that advice in the last couple of years. Consultant stations are now running stories much longer than they formerly did, and an emphasis on hard-nosed investigative reporting is emerging, together with less conviction on the consultants' part that news about government is automatically dull.

Ames, Iowa

There is great competition for ratings in all TV programming with special emphasis on news, since broadcasters believe good news ratings lead to good prime-time ratings. Local news has become profitable and that has added intensity to the competition. None of this, however, has led to better news coverage. Stories get shorter all the time and the stations don't want to report anything without tape or film. The idea is to get ratings, to have the most popular anchors and "news team"—a pet phrase— not to enlighten the public. There are exceptions from time to time, of course, but timidity and fear of offending viewers, combined with many broadcast journalists who are committed to being "well-known broadcasters" more than to being journalists, make local newscasting rather shallow, narrow and personality-oriented. There are many young reporters—some skillful, but still glossy in approach. They are not piercing or seasoned and they may suit the tastes of this area, but they rock no boats.

Memphis, Tennessee

Broadcast journalism during the past ten years has been going fast, sideways. We do not go up, we do not have depth, but we sprawl all over. We have more stations, more people, more money, but it does not add up to more quality. We are always covering news that has been found by someone else. We forever explain the unexplainable to a mass audience, who, if they happen to be paying attention, get something they think is accurate. Why? Because they see us or hear us and we look sincere. If we don't look sincere, or interesting, or sound right, we are shunted aside for someone who has personality. We are not as well off, in many regards, as we were in the best days of radio. Then we had comment by people who knew what was happening and kept informed about it. News was evaluated on what its significance was, not on its picture possibilities.

Sacramento, California

Network ownership still did not guarantee quality in the local news product. Owned-and-operated stations in New York and Los Angeles, the two most important and most lucrative markets in the nation, remained far from the top of the list of big market stations in the distinction of their journalistic achievements. The Du-Pont-Columbia correspondent reported recently from Los Angeles:

> The minute local television management discovered the news could be a big money maker, the journalists were kicked out and the entertainment oriented general managers made major decisions regarding talent, budget, sets and the like. That meant disaster for local television news in Los Angeles. As ratings fell, it got worse. The higher the ratings, the less interference. When CBS' KNXT began to fall in the ratings, panic set in and non-journalists set about destroying a reputation built up over a decade. KNXT is still in sub-third place (independents screening situation comedies and dramas beat it out on occasion). Now the same thing appears to be happening to KNBC. As KABC continues to hold a lead (with a combination of show-biz, self-help and personality journalism), KNBC is starting to show the signs of losing the battle. Entertainment, based on faltering ratings, not news decisions, is slowly changing KNBC from a responsible news operation into a "let's-do-what-KABC-does" copycat.

The L.A. correspondent also spotted another trend in local news that he considered prevalent enough to be ominous:

The hiring of professionals to take the place of reporters; by professionals, I mean doctors, lawyers, stockbrokers, psychiatrists, astrologers and the like—biased members of a particular profession reporting on that profession. . . . The danger, of course, is that these people . . . whose first allegiance is to their profession, not to the public, are replacing general assignment and specialized television/radio reporters. So instead of having a reporter who is primarily interested in the public good reporting on medical health news, you have a member of the medical profession, usually endorsed and supported by the local medical association, doing the job. Double that when you talk about business news. Triple it when you talk about legal matters. Then add former politicians covering political events, former ball players covering sports, former diplomats covering international events—and you have news reported in a certain way by people who put their profession above their "journalism."

The news and public affairs documentary on local television and radio in the past decade was having as hard a time as its equivalent at the networks. As local broadcast journalists grew in the expertise and intelligence required to put together an extended essay on an important subject, the time and budgets for such concerted attempts at excellence were slowly being cut back or removed entirely.*

Thirty-seven percent of the correspondents report-

---

*In September 1979, WCBS-TV, the flagship station of the CBS-TV network, dropped its hard-hitting local documentary series *Eye On,* produced by Morton Silverstein ("Banks and the Poor"). Its nonfiction replacement, sharing the prime-time access slot with *The Muppets* and *The Gong Show,* was a new soft feature magazine called *Real Life!*

ing to the Survey noted a decline in the number of documentaries getting on the air in their communities. In their place was a dramatic rise in the number of mini-documentaries strung through regular newscasts reported in 83 percent of the same communities.

In some cases these fragmented series added up to worthwhile coverage of such substantial topics as nuclear power, mass transit, inflation, civil rights, and hazardous wastes. However, frequent and more sensational topics for local mini-documentaries reported by station news directors included teenage prostitution and pregnancy, homosexuality, wife and child abuse, drugs, violent crime, and incest.

These obvious appeals to the morbid interests of the stations' target audiences were habitually run during the ratings sweeps periods, which determined the prices management could charge for the subsequent quarter's commercials. That ratings were figuring increasingly in their editorial decisions was admitted by two out of three news directors reporting to the Survey.

At the beginning of the decade, half the entrants in the DuPont-Columbia Awards competition aspired, admittedly with widely varying degrees of success, to emulate the best of network TV journalism represented in the traditional thirty-minute and hour-long documentary. At the end of the decade, with the ability to produce network quality essays, the aspiration had dwindled away with only a small proportion of stations coast to coast regularly producing this classic broadcast form. At the top of this list, in addition to the examples already cited, were:

• "Joe McCarthy: An American Ism," a striking portrait of the renegade Wisconsin senator in the testimony of friends and acquaintances put together for WHA Madison.

• KUTV Salt Lake City's "Clouds of Doubt," which examined the perils of low-level radiation from the revealing standpoint of residents of a state where atomic fallout for a long time was a frequent occurrence.

• KTCA/KTCI Saint Paul's "Power Play," an exploration of the conflict over the high-tension power lines looping across the Midwest, and why or why not they should be there.

• KING Seattle's "Columbia: A River of Lakes," a stunning historical trip down one of the nation's great rivers, which included a thorough inquiry into the environmental challenges faced in the past century.

• KDIN Des Moines' "Camp Sunnyside," a beautifully photographed, scored, and edited vignette on a summer camp for handicapped people in the bucolic Iowa countryside.

Next to the mini-documentaries, which siphoned off budget and staff and subject matter from traditional documentaries, were the TV magazines. In the Survey's first year, KHOU-TV Houston reported:

> In February we initiated a monthly half-hour program called *30 Minutes,* patterned after the CBS *60 Minutes.* It's a magazine format show and enables us to do an investigative reporting job on any subject and still include something "upbeat" within the same show.

This was the only magazine show which surfaced in that year's roundup. By the season of 1978–79, nine out of every ten stations reporting to the Survey had some variety of TV magazine. The trend—led by Group W's

highly successful weekday half-hour *Evening* (also
called *P.M.*) and by late 1979 seen five evenings a week
in fifty-one markets—was toward personality, consumer services, and other "upbeat" items. Still, there
was a growing number of stations that included hard
news and investigative features, sometimes devoting
their full time to a single story, among them energy,
mass transportation, nuclear power, and health.

Despite the ups and downs of local news and public
affairs, 81 percent of those most concerned—the station
news directors—declared themselves hopeful for the
future of their art. But their comments indicated that
although there were many small victories the battle for
quality journalism was far from won.

> We keep our stories short, but on occasion we
> have devoted as much as ten minutes in a news-
> cast to one subject. These include a city police
> strike, the sudden death of our Congressman,
> and Three Mile Island. We have a policy, newly
> adopted in 1978, which allows the entire news-
> cast to be devoted to one subject if warranted.
>
> *Hagerstown, Maryland*

> Someone said TV newscasts are beginning to
> sound and look like "top 40" disc jockey shows.
> They may be right. Producers demand 90-
> second story time and call it a big event. Some
> stations are even running silent tape and film
> stories in the window behind the anchor with
> 10 seconds of copy. Isn't that dandy? Too many
> TV newscasts are taking the "popcorn" ap-
> proach, all fluff and no substance. Who cares
> that the consumer's taxes are going up . . . that
> his wife will be paying 25 more cents for a half-

gallon of milk? Judging from some of the nightly newscasts . . . apparently not a soul. The attitude today seems to be . . . "give 'em rape, murder and floods, but don't give the viewer anything that requires some thinking."

Reno, Nevada

The credibility of broadcast journalism suffers most from its failure to probe deeply, with clarity, into everything being covered. There is still too much emphasis on the cosmetics of broadcast journalism and not enough on the substance of what is being reported. We frequently fail to determine what is important to the viewer or listener and then present it in a form and language that is relevant to him. We have done little to bolster audience confidence that we are honest, unbiased and fair.

Portland, Oregon

While there are many clouds on our horizon, it is a challenge to fight the growing problems of our profession. The opportunity still remains to inform and illuminate if we so choose. But there still is the chance for everything to go down the drain if reporters succumb to consultants and less-than-competent management. The fight is continuing.

Columbus, Ohio

Two years ago, I worked at a small market station that was going places. Now, I'm at a large market station standing still. Managements seem less willing to spend money for quality news operations. And the trend in news presentations is leaning more toward slickness with less substance.

Thank God for the occasional station that still does it right.

Minneapolis, Minnesota

I believe the stakes involved in the issues we are compelled to cover are reaching such high levels and that the complexity of the issues on which those stakes rest have become so deep that we may well end by alienating huge blocks of people, no matter how fair the coverage, and may soon find fairness eluding us because of our inability to deal adequately with issues of pressing magnitude in the framework we must work in.

Eugene, Oregon

In some cases, broadcast journalism is very good. It brings out elements of stories that can be told in no other way. Its impact can be profound. Most of the time (90 percent) I am not pleased with what I see. From New York to Denver to Boise, the local news is terrible. The stories are predictable, the treatments are uninspired, the journalism is weak. People in this industry don't seem to be concerned with more than the "who," "what," and "when." Where are the local stations who break their budgets providing the "how" and "why"? Where are the local reporters who really research their stories, really try to make them meaningful? And, just as importantly, where are the editors and news directors who insist upon it?

Seattle, Washington

Local news has changed from being an FCC commitment to becoming the very frontispiece of the station and single most important area of concern. This has manifested itself in the growth and size of newsroom staff, as well as money invested and increased maturity in news service provided to viewers. Investigative teams, specialty reporters and advanced equipment are all part of today's newsroom operation.

Philadelphia, Pennsylvania

Ten years ago the station had two full-time news people and a daily news audience of 8,500 households. News now has 20 people and an audience of 118,000 households a day. It is really an incomparable situation.

Jonesboro, Arkansas

The most dramatic change has been the improved profitability and local demand for quality news on television. This situation has allowed for substantial news staff development and equipment acquisition. A change has taken place in station programming priorities with a sharp impact on the informative sources of our community.

Asheville, North Carolina

I just resigned over an ethical dilemma and have decided to leave broadcast journalism. As a result, I am a poor witness.

Albany, New York

It is amazing that an industry/profession has managed to grow from nothing to Goliath in 25 years . . . and manages to do so with so little experimentation and daring.

New York, New York

When I came six years ago, the market was far less sophisticated than its size would suggest. There was heavy emphasis on short anchor voice-over film stories on wrecks, fires, and stories that had no wide influence on the audience. We instituted beat reporting and started doing series. We hired consumer, medical, and arts reporters. We traveled from coast to coast on special assignments. We started breaking stories before the newspapers. They now monitor our broadcast to insure they aren't missing a big story.

Dallas, Texas

An absolute explosion of people and money— primarily in the news magazine and documentary- film areas. Our station has gone from now-and- then success to a year when we swept the awards . . . but more importantly, we've begun to have an impact in this area. Our programs are watched, criticized, praised, and requested by legislators, community groups, and other interested parties. The station management (largely because of the success) has been supportive.

Seattle, Washington

In addition to basic equipment and personnel improvements, the most dramatic change has been in emphasis. Reporters are no longer mouth- pieces for local bureaucrats and political figures, but are now enterprising and investigating and using the medium to its best advantage. We are looking at our reporting effort in terms of what it means to our viewers/listeners and how what we do helps to benefit them. We have come a long way in making the market more competitive, which, in the long run, benefits those we serve.

Rock Island, Illinois

5/Foreign News

In the 1968–69 season the Czech crisis was the overseas story that received the most extensive coverage, giving the networks an opportunity to take full advantage of the recently expanded capabilities of satellite transmissions. The events in Prague arrived on the nation's home screens with a remarkable if painful clarity. For the majority of Americans, and for the newspeople reporting back to them, there was no question about which side to root and mourn for. The same clarity seemed to illumine the Arab-Israeli conflict, a continuing concern of the network evening news in the period following the Seven Day War. These stories, and the coverage of President Nixon's overseas travels, the Paris peace talks, the Pope in Bogotá, the French elections, and the 1968 Olympics, all brought to televiewers by satellite, gave little indication of the part broadcast news was to play on the world stage as the decade came to an end.

The great days of UN coverage had long since passed, and international stories pursued at length—which might have revealed the dim lineaments of major stories to come—were few and far between.

In the first season in which the DuPont-Columbia Survey kept score, there were—in addition to takeouts on the Czech crisis—an NBC hour devoted to Russia in the Mediterranean, a two-hour special on "China Today and Tomorrow," and a half-hour special on France after de Gaulle. CBS had a half-hour program on Cuba, and it devoted a prime-time hour to the Paris peace talks and an hour to the Japanese. ABC scheduled two hours, one on Soviet soldiers, the other on the Middle East. With all the world to cover, this was a meager helping to serve to the nation's prime-time audience.

The practice of taking extended stories on breaking foreign news and then relegating them to the far end of the broadcast schedule, where audiences and time charges were small, began early in the decade and persisted to the end.

Always considering the limited time at their disposal and the world they had to cover, the network evening newscasts did a praiseworthy job of keeping on top of hard news developments abroad. Unfortunately these offerings, depending on the circumstances of the viewer and the information available from other sources, usually seemed either too much or too little. Still, the big stories were there—Chile, China, Bangladesh—handled with care and caution if not with the detail they deserved. Most of the possibilities for foreign "actualities" that might open daytime and prime-time television to reality remained untouched.

Ten years later, the box score for foreign news was little improved. With a half hour allotted to cover the world each night, the network newscasts were still scrambling to touch a fraction of the stories that needed covering and were lingering over only the most compelling. During the season of 1978–79, the networks offered prime-time documentaries on exactly five foreign subjects. Among the best were "The Battle for South Africa," one of Bill Moyers's last contributions to CBS before returning to PBS, which was aired on Labor Day weekend, and Ed Bradley's "The Boat People" (also for CBS), which, however moving, was stronger on desperate effects than on causes and cures. ABC's long-running religious series, *Directions,* presented some of the most knowledgeable international reporting of the year with striking segments on the Middle East, the Philippines under martial law, and the strife in Honduras and Ireland. On PBS, the *World* series, produced by a consortium of talents in western Europe and Canada in conjunction with Boston station WGBH, did a particularly perceptive job in its multinational story "F-16: Sale of the Century."

In addition to six hours of prime-time documentaries on foreign subjects, the networks devoted another four prime-time hours to special reports on overseas stories and relegated even more time (13 hours) to the stretch after the local late-night news—when affiliate clearance regularly ran below the prime-time level. Live network cameras were never seen at the United Nations during the 1978–79 broadcast year, and live coverage of overseas stories occurred just three times during the year,* none in prime-time evening hours. This made all the more remarkable the increasing part throughout the decade that TV news was perceived to have in the course of international affairs.

*Exclusive of those concerning the papal successions (and Christmas Eve at the Vatican) which were massively covered by all three networks.

The most dramatic and clear-cut example occurred in November 1977, when so-called "TV diplomacy" appeared on the scene as an important component in the ongoing Arab-Israeli talks. The shuttling back and forth of top network newspeople, and their courting by the heads of state of the two nations, led Israeli commentator Mark Segal to say in *Variety:*

> The politics as entertainment syndrome appears to be taking over the most fateful discussions in Middle East history.... Begin seems to be enjoying all the razzmatazz as much as Sadat.... That they have appointed Barbara Walters as the major oracle of Middle East diplomacy hardly adds to the solemnity of their purpose.... The unrealistic expectation that decades of bloodshed and hostility can be made to vanish by some magic television wand is, perhaps, the result of the way Begin has allowed Sadat, as part of his bid to win over U.S. public opinion, to convert the negotiating process into part of the American TV networks' competition for placement in the ratings.*

Flora Lewis of the *New York Times* did not concur:

> To consider the new technique a matter of show business or personal vanity would be a serious mistake. It has already proven highly effective in the Middle East. And the chances are that it will gradually be taken up for use in other areas, where

*Sadat and Begin were not the only ones blamed for using the press to achieve their ends. In March 1979, press secretary Jody Powell and media adviser Gerald Rafshoon were accused of tricking the press into believing that the continuing peace talks were doomed in order, according to one correspondent, "to manipulate the American people through the news media to put pressure on the Israelis."

matters of tremendous importance to billions of people are still kept secret until there is a result, a decision or an agreement.

In effect, mass diplomacy has become a tool of negotiations. While there has not yet been a result in the Middle East talks, there has already been a tangible impact. . . .

Once the American people had become engaged in the action, through Sadat's policy of granting frequent interviews and making himself continuously visible, it did become important for Mr. Begin to win his share of interest and support being generated. . . .

Without spending a penny in this way, Mr. Sadat has induced the world's most powerful media to run to him and publicize what he has to say. He has managed to begin mass diplomacy.

And while it may take some time before other leaders achieve his instinctive grasp of how to handle it, the new method is almost certainly here to stay, as long as the new technology of communications exists.

Although the ultimate outcome, a confirmed treaty, was still awaited, the TV-inspired Sadat-Begin talks did lead to Camp David and the surge of hope that followed, visibly communicated in one of the decade's most moving passages of broadcast journalism.

An even more dramatic and disturbing example of broadcasting's sudden involvement in the affairs of nations awaited TV's coverage of another Middle Eastern nation. In the early months of 1978, when the prerevolution crisis in Iran was well under way, network evening newscasts gave no indication of the situation. The first mention came on May 11, an ABC report that an anti-Shah demonstration had been stopped in a major show of force by the Iranian army. Three days later, CBS reported that a strike was planned, and NBC noted briefly that riots had been broken up. In all of June and July—as the crisis escalated—there was a single reference to Iran: an NBC report of a heat wave in the country. In mid-August there was a sprinkling of reports on bombings, riots, and demonstrations. In September the first background pieces appeared, including an ABC interview with the Shah and his newly appointed prime minister in which they both pledged to end the turmoil. By November the three networks had begun broadcasting reports at least every other day dispatched from correspondents freshly arrived in Iran, where the last permanent U.S. news bureau, that of *The New York Times,* had been closed in February 1977.

It was no secret that the networks—and most American news organizations—had overlooked some important developments. Dick Fischer, NBC's executive vice-president for news, admitted to *Time* magazine, "Early on, we reported softly on the Shah; we thought he was our man."

In January and February, as the situation evolved into a full-fledged revolution, U.S. journalists with their backpacks, cameras, and microphones frequently found themselves targeted as the most conspicuous representatives of a suddenly unpopular nation. According to critic Ron Powers, writing in *TV Guide:*

> No armed conflict in recent world history—not even Vietnam—posed such a variety of extreme dangers to the journalists covering it (especially Americans). No member of the American broadcast corps was killed, although several were beaten

and threatened. And yet the hazards faced by TV correspondents and technicians were almost perversely chilling.

Said NBC's Robert Hager, "Clearly our government, our State Department, were not taking Khomeini seriously enough. We could see an optimism coming out of State that just wasn't supportable. People tend to criticize television news for covering the story in the streets. In this case the story was in the streets."

The coverage the networks gave in their scramble to catch up ended by pleasing no one. The Carter administration was reported infuriated, with Jody Powell stating that network reports of unauthorized and often contradictory statements from unnamed administration officials "have probably done more damage to American interests than any organized anti-American forces in Iran."

The other side was even less enthusiastic. A self-styled spokesman for the Iranian revolutionaries indicated their sense of unfairness and affront. Pointing out to the editors of *The New York Times* the past indifference of the U.S. press to the atrocities perpetrated by the Shah, the writer, Michael Parenti, a visiting Fellow at the Institute for Policy Studies, went on:

> Now the furies of revolution have lashed back, thus far executing about 200 of the Shah's henchmen—less than what the Savak would arrest and torture on a slow weekend. And now the U.S. press has suddenly become acutely concerned, keeping a careful count of the "victims," printing photos of firing squads and making repeated references to the "revulsion" and "outrage" felt by anonymous "middle class" Iranians who apparently are en-

dowed with finer sensibilities than the mass of ordinary people who bore the brunt of the Shah's repression. At the same time, American commentators are quick to observe that the new regime is merely replacing the one repression with another.

So it has always been with the recording of revolutions: the mass of nameless innocents victimized by the *ancien régime* go uncounted and unnoticed, but when the not-so-innocent murderers are brought to revolutionary justice, the business-owned press is suddenly filled with references to "brutality" and "cruelty." That anyone could equate the horrors of the Shah's regime with the ferment, change and struggle that is going on in Iran today is a tribute to the biases of the U.S. press, a press that has learned to treat the atrocities of the U.S.-supported right-wing regimes with benign neglect while casting a stern, self-righteous eye on the popular revolutions that challenge such regimes.

If Iran during January and February represented the severest risk to U.S. journalists to date, worse was to come nine months later, when the U.S. embassy was occupied and sixty-two hostages taken, an act approved by the country's new leader, Ayatollah Ruhollah Khomeini. And yet, as the last Americans fled the hostile nation, with the remaining five hundred shrinking to a handful, the network presence steadily increased. Soon more than sixty staff members from the three networks moved through the mobs that burned American flags, shook their fists, and shouted to the camera, "Death to Carter and all Americans."*

*On January 15, 1980, the ruling Revolutionary Council ordered all American journalists out of Iran.

On November 18, at the height of the terror, three network newsmen (Mike Wallace of CBS, John Hart of NBC, and Peter Jennings of ABC) were given safe passage to the sacred city of Qum and allowed access to Ayatollah Khomeini. Mike Wallace explained the ground rules to viewers of *60 Minutes* that evening:

> No question could be asked unless it was approved ahead of time. No questions about Iran's internal politics. No questions about a lack of freedom under the Ayatollah. But there seemed no pattern to those questions that were disallowed; about half of those we proposed were simply forbidden. The interpreter said he would refuse even to ask the Ayatollah any questions that he, the interpreter, deemed inappropriate.

Even with such disclaimers, and despite the reporters' deferential manner, the questions had a provocative sound as the Ayatollah listened with a stern, unsmiling face and gave his emphatic replies.

> WALLACE: Do you still say, Imam, that if the Shah —the ex-Shah—is not returned to Iran, that those American hostages in the American embassy compound will not be freed?
>
> AYATOLLAH: . . . Unless he is returned, the hostages will not be freed.

Before the three interviews were over, the Iranian leader had been asked, among other things, if he considered himself at war with the United States; if he intended to kill the hostages, or, if not, how long they would be kept in captivity; if he would be willing to meet Carter in a third country or, alternatively, to take the matter before the United Nations. The answers were either noncommittal or negative.

Wallace reminded the Ayatollah that President Carter had accused him of terrorism and that President Sadat of Egypt, "a devoutly religious man, a Moslem, says that what you are doing now is—quote—'a disgrace to Islam.' And he calls you, Imam—forgive me, his words, not mine—'a lunatic.' " In response, the Ayatollah demanded that the Egyptian people overthrow Sadat as the Iranians had the Shah.

If the viewers wondered what the diplomats, apparently superseded and outflanked, were doing while this was going on, Richard Valeriani—following the John Hart interview on *Prime Time Sunday*—told them, "The administration . . . is getting information from the networks. . . . They don't have that kind of contact with the Ayatollah themselves."*

---

*Some indication of how well informed the Ayatollah was on U.S. TV news was given on the *MacNeil/Lehrer Report* the following evening when Robert MacNeil, who had given the Ayatollah his first extended exposure on American TV in an interview from Paris the previous December, concluded a broadcast on "Who Gets Hurt in the Economic War Between the U.S. and Iran":

". . . I'd just like to give you a personal note to explain why you did not see an interview with Ayatollah Khomeini on the *MacNeil/-Lehrer Report.* We were told last Wednesday that the Ayatollah would give us an exclusive interview. I left immediately for Teheran with two members of our staff, and we arrived there Thursday evening.

"On Friday, the day we expected to tape a one-hour interview, we were told they'd decided to give interviews to all the American networks over the weekend. We concluded that four American television interviews with the Ayatollah was journalistic overkill and made no sense for public television, competitively or financially. The commercial networks taped their interviews Sunday morning; we decided not to join them. In the end, knowing the restrictions they had to work under, it seemed certain that we

On Thanksgiving Day, Foreign Minister Abolhasson Bani Sadr told a gathering of journalists, "We need to convey our message to the world. . . . For this we must use the media. . . . What we want from you is nothing but the revelation of truth to the world. . . . Don't you want this world problem to be the first one that is solved by reporters?"

That TV's intrusion in Iran seemed questionable was not just because the United States was a principal in the negotiations and that the outcome could be a matter of life and death, if not war, although that certainly had to be a major consideration. Reinforcing this anxiety was the memory of two other recent and disastrous incidents involving adventurous TV journalists outside the continental borders of the United States.

First in point of time had been the events at Jonestown in Guyana, where reporter Don Harris and several others were gunned down following a provocative interview with cult leader Jim Jones. With a dark irony, the murder of Harris and the mass suicides that followed had taken place exactly a year before the network reporters arrived at Qum, and they were being recapitulated on the same newscasts that reported the confrontation with the Ayatollah. This juxtaposition made the superficial similarities between the two encounters—a fanatic being faced by a persistent, fear-

---

would not have been able to get the kind of extended, in-depth interview we strive for on this program.

"As any reporter will tell you, it's very disappointing to be so close to a big scoop and have it evaporate, but that's what happens sometimes."

The Ayatollah had not only snubbed his old friends at PBS but had allotted the top-rated *60 Minutes* first place and a full hour, while the other two networks had to be content with fifteen minutes each.

less, and possibly indiscreet reporter, difficult to ignore. The fact that Jim Jones represented a congregation of 900 hundred suicidal souls, while the Ayatollah ruled over a nation of 35 million potential martyrs, offered little reassurance.

Equally disturbing was the recent memory of the Nicaraguan revolution and the fate of ABC-TV correspondent Bill Stewart, casually murdered on camera by one of dictator Anastasio Somoza Debayle's national guardsmen. The crime presented on the ABC evening news as a 30-second vignette had dramatic consequences in the reversal of U.S. foreign policy and the final downfall of Nicaragua's long-term leader.

The three network correspondents withdrew from the Ayatollah's stronghold safely, and in apparent good order. However, they left behind them the impression that several diplomatic options had been quickly and finally disposed of by amateurs. This suspicion hovered over subsequent interviews with the revolutionary students, and with the formidable Sadegh Ghotbzadeh, who appropriately was the director of Iran's state television before the Ayatollah chose him as his third foreign minister.*

This impression of dangerous meddling was underscored by off-the-record comments made by Hodding Carter of the State Department, who told a group of Princeton University students, "In one damn set of interviews, a rigid statement was set down on the inevitability of trials for our people. It put into concrete what

*Ghotbzadeh allegedly got rid of his predecessor, Mehdi Bazargan, by broadcasting a tape of him shaking hands with Zbigniew Brzezinski in Algiers.

could have been dismissed as a muttering behind closed doors."

The networks took violent exception to Carter's aspersions. NBC News President William J. Small said, "Hodding Carter has handled a most difficult job exceedingly well. Our reporters have handled a similar job brilliantly. I would suggest Mr. Carter stick to his job—we to ours." CBS News President Bill Leonard wrote Carter, "The news divisions of the networks should be thanked—not criticized—for bringing this planned action to light at the earliest time possible, thereby allowing the negotiating process now under way to have begun as soon as possible." And ABC News President Roone Arledge said, "Short of not reporting Khomeini's statements or submitting to your censorship, I believe we acted responsibly. I reject completely your thesis to the contrary."

Three days later, another hassle developed when NBC chose to accept the revolutionaries' offer of an interview with one of the imprisoned marines. CBS and ABC had rejected the offer on the grounds that to accede to the revolutionaries' conditions concerning editing and the airing of a long-winded statement defining their position would be unacceptable journalistic practice. Roone Arledge commented, "It was not television's proudest moment. I don't know how much harm it did to television journalism to have one of the networks knowingly participate in the students' quest for a forum. It's a setback for those of us trying to operate responsibly in a sensitive terrain." Bill Leonard said, "As long as they were dictating the spokesman, the cameras, the hostage, and when we could televise it, they were asking us to be a conduit rather than a journalistic organization. I didn't spend three seconds with that decision."

But NBC News President William J. Small saw it differently. "We did it because it was a very important interview, because no one has talked to any of these hostages for thirty-five days. The American public has the right to know what's going on there. Obviously, we knew we'd have to do it in the presence of the students. They're not going to let you take a hostage home for Christmas. I don't know what better proof there is of its importance than the page-one play it got in newspapers across the country. For all the criticism, I'd do it again tonight—no question about it." He went on, "If you look at the history of kidnap victims and hostages generally, one of the things you realize is that if there were a total news blackout the people holding these hostages would do something more dramatic. Coverage is the escape valve for steam. I'm not saying that we're trying to be an escape valve—that's not our mission, even if it serves that purpose."

The New York Times came to NBC's defense editorially:

> In the current flap, the question has become who is using whom, and for what? To the Carter Administration, it seemed wrong for NBC to interview one hostage, who may have been under duress. Others question whether NBC was right to agree to broadcast the interview in prime time and to permit an accompanying statement of Iran's case. White House Press Secretary Jody Powell called the interview "a cruel and cynical attempt" by Iran to divert public attention. What also seemed to trouble Mr. Powell was that Iran

tried to use American television to its own advantage.

American television, in doing its job, may at times serve Iranian government purposes. It may at times serve American government purposes. But throughout, it serves American *public* purposes as well. The public needs to understand Iranian passions, real as well as staged. The public is not, in any case, so gullible as to swallow any Iranian argument whole; if anything, the various televised appearances of Iranian leaders have strengthened American resolve. . . .

American journalists have not sought a diplomatic role in Iran. It has been thrust upon them. Those covering Iran have been under pressure from two sets of would-be official editors, Iranian and American. At some point, timidity or competitive zeal might indeed impel a network or newspaper to shave professional standards. But the networks have on the whole held to the obligation of deciding, independently, what is newsworthy. The lesson is the same as always: The only duty the media can effectively perform is their own.

On Christmas Day, the Iranian captors offered the networks color film taken during the visit of four clergymen to the hostages. The film contained statements that were critical of the Shah and of U.S. policy toward Iran. The captors insisted that the film be shown in its entirety, without prescreening. The networks refused the offer. The captors later withdrew their preconditions, and segments of the film ran on news programs over all three networks on December 31.

By mid-December, all three network newscasts had led with the Iran story for well over a month, with coverage frequently accounting for well over half their allotted time. Although there were no prime-time programs, 46 late-night specials were aired in the same period, 35 on ABC, 6 on NBC, and 5 on CBS. The weekend network panel shows for six weeks allotted 50 percent of their time solely to Iran-related interviews. The *MacNeil/Lehrer Report* devoted an unprecedented string of sixteen programs in six weeks to commentary and explanation of the Iran crisis.*

Not only was legitimate broadcast news coverage setting records for attention to a single subject, parajournalism was deep into the act as well. In six weeks, *Good Morning, America* devoted all but two days of its daily public affairs segment to Iran, for a total of five hours of coverage. International diplomats were interviewed, as were American politicians, and a psychologist who discussed the effects of being held hostage.

The *Today* show carried Iran-related interviews at least every other day, twice giving over the entire first half hour to the situation in Iran. Talk shows and phone-ins were swamped with people wanting to express their opinions. Typical was WRC, NBC's owned-and-operated all-talk radio station in the nation's capital, where the average of two hundred calls an hour went up to two thousand. A disconcerting commentary on the whole bloodcurdling sequence was offered on day 33 of the embassy occupation. After a month of intercepting screamed imprecations and unveiled threats, Tom Fenton, CBS senior European correspondent on the scene, contributed a three-minute *Evening News*

---

*No network chose to interrupt its prime-time schedule to cover the critical meetings at the UN Security Council at the beginning of December.

feature on the lot of the journalist in Iran, which included an acknowledgment that the student revolutionaries were "very savvy kids" and that "It didn't take them long to realize that this is a media event."

However expert and cynical the revolutionaries had become in their handling of the media, it was hard to dismiss such coverage as overkill. A big story got big attention—and for that, one had to be grateful. Still, it was difficult to reconcile this sudden and massive commitment with the day-to-day scanting that the circumstances of broadcast journalism dictated in the area of international news.* Whatever the next flash point in the world might be, it was likely that U.S. broadcast journalists, dedicated though they might be, would be working at a handicap in arriving late on the scene, scrambling to catch up with their explanations as to exactly what was going on and why, and leaving the follow-up to others once the action moved elsewhere.

*For a consideration of the administrative problems of foreign coverage, see the report by Jan Stone, "The Picture from Abroad," in Part III.

6/Comings and Goings

Probably in no field more than foreign affairs was the decline of the broadcast commentator more conspicuous. If TV had never achieved the distinction and diversity in commentary that was characteristic of radio in its prime, it had still boasted a few outspoken and articulate opinion molders at the beginning of the 1970s. By the decade's end, Eric Sevareid had been forced to retire from CBS at a vigorous sixty-five, David Brinkley had been downgraded at NBC, and even Shana Alexander and Jack Kilpatrick had been deprived of their brief allotment on *60 Minutes*.

But perhaps most discouraging was the departure of Howard K. Smith. Smith, whose commentaries in recent years had been among the most outspoken on the air, posted a parting memo, "To my friends and colleagues at ABC News," which read:

> I have heard some rumors about my future relations with ABC, and I know no way to clear them up but to place this note where anyone who wishes may read it:

ABC News informed me some time ago that they would like to negotiate a new contract to replace my seven-year contract which expires June 1. They have now made it clear, however, that my commentary on the Evening News would not be part of the offer, for it is to be ended "to lighten the show."

They have been so hazy about what I would do that it sounds increasingly to me like a job without a real function. I cannot agree to a contract which does not offer me a genuine opportunity to practice my craft.

With great regret, therefore, I have written a letter to our boss saying I have decided to leave ABC. With time so short I must try now to find another professional outlet. I hope I will succeed.

This has been a painful decision, for I have deep roots at ABC and many friendships I hate to see grow tenuous by my absence. I shall remember you and our many shared times of troubles fondly.

The fact that Smith had been released by the highly competitive and image-conscious ABC news operation and was not replaced did not bode well for the future of the useful and important vocation of broadcast commentator. Nor did the fate of Rod MacLeish, who had been hired away from Group W in 1977 as a possible replacement for Sevareid and was still waiting in the wings at CBS, offering his articulate and intelligent commentaries to radio listeners.*

The disappearance of major journalistic talent or its underutilization was a recurrent phenomenon in news

---

*John Chancellor, rumored to be anxious to get into commentary and at one time mentioned as Sevareid's replacement, was still in his anchor spot at NBC in the 1979–80 season.

and public affairs broadcasting during the decade. These departures frequently followed the airing of controversial programs. Among those lost to the networks or all but ignored by them were Peter Davis ("The Selling of the Pentagon") and Marty Carr ("Hunger in America," "Migrant," "This Child Is Rated X"). The lot of independent producers in news and public affairs had been a matter of growing concern even as their expertise and authority grew.

The position of men standing at the top of the network news operations seemed as precarious as those they hired and fired. Within a three-year span, NBC had replaced Richard Wald as news president with Lester Crystal, who himself was replaced before his second season was finished by Dick Salant's choice, William Small. At CBS, sixty-three-year-old Bill Leonard was a lame-duck replacement for Salant, with a new head scheduled to be brought in before April 1981. A period of great turmoil and changes in executive structure had preceded the elevation of Roone Arledge to president of ABC News, and the shifts and additions, among them NBC's Wald, continued long after his arrival on the scene.

At the beginning of the decade, all three network news operations had been in old experienced hands. At the end, with their responsibilities escalating, top news executives were being replaced with increasing frequency.

7/Government

Electoral politics, already touched on in chapter 1, were the most superficial expression of the last decade's acutely uncomfortable and yet apparently symbiotic relationship between government and broadcasting.

During this time, the confrontation unquestionably had its most dramatic expression in the alliterative attacks of Spiro Agnew, and then the debacle of Watergate. It was the decade of "The Selling of the Pentagon," which put the late Representative F. Edward Hebert (D. La.) on the home-screen coast to coast saying, "I'm one of those who believe that the most vicious instrument in America today is network television." The same program led CBS President Frank Stanton to risk the penitentiary by defying a congressional subpoena and forcing his adversary—Representative Harley Staggers (D. W.Va.)—to back down. It was the decade of the Public Broadcasting Service's "Banks and the Poor," a no-holds-barred indictment of the financial status quo that ended with a list of 133 government officials who might possibly be suspected of conflict of interest in the matter of money-lending but unquestionably were responsible for voting essential funds to the entities that produced and put the program on the air. It was the decade of the Pentagon Papers, the Pike Report on the CIA, and "presidential enemy" Daniel Schorr's eloquent defense of the First Amendment in the presence of his congressional critics a few days before he took permanent leave of his uneasy network bosses.

It was the decade when Justice Lewis F. Powell, Jr., just prior to his nomination to the Supreme Court, suggested:

> The national television networks should be monitored in the same way that textbooks should be kept under constant surveillance. This applies not merely to so-called educational programs (such as "The Selling of the Pentagon") but to the daily "news analysis," which so often includes the most insidious type of criticism of the enterprise system. . . .
>
> This monitoring, to be effective, would require constant examination of the texts of adequate samples of programs. Complaints—to the media and to the Federal Communications Commission— should be made promptly and strongly when programs are unfair or inaccurate.

And it was a time when acting FBI chief L. Patrick Gray 3d asked, after viewing a segment of *60 Minutes* on the Law Enforcement Assistance Administration:

> Is the other side of the coin—the free press that should keep the electorate informed—now stepping into a new role—that of controlling the electorate by controlling the information it receives? Instead of the public using the press as the source of its information, is the process now being re-

versed, so that the press will be using the public in the same way that a programmer uses a computer? . . . There is a crisis of confidence in the press.

The reason for this inability of government and broadcasting to settle their differences, or at least ignore each other, obviously came from the broadcasters' enormous importance as a purveyor of information, of news and public affairs. If broadcasting had been simply a matter of entertainment or even, as some contended, the accumulating and selling of audiences, its relationship with the government and its representatives, elected or appointed, would have presented no more prickly problems than any other highly competitive and profitable enterprise, say the movie or record or even publishing industries.

But broadcasting depended on a limited resource that from the start had been acknowledged to belong to the public—the air. Because of this it was licensed, a fact that did not apply to other informational media. The hybrid nature of the medium and its statutory responsibilities to "the public interest, convenience, and necessity" not only made it a continual provocation and temptation to the politically entrenched but presented regulatory problems that persisted and grew throughout the decade.

The deregulation of radio and TV was already a familiar cry in 1968, when the DuPont-Columbia Survey began its coverage of the Washington scene. One part of the justification for lifting licenses was commercial: Was it tolerable, although the broadcasters got their franchises for little or nothing and had become rich exercising them, that they be subject to the possibility of challenge and loss? The other part was philosophical-constitutional: Wasn't licensing the nation's prime news source an infringement of important rights and a violation of the First Amendment?

In 1969, Senator John Pastore, chairman of the Communications Subcommittee of the Senate Commerce Committee, and twenty of his colleagues in the Senate had sponsored a bill, S.2004, which according to those opposed would have effectively given broadcasters their franchises in perpetuity. Eighty almost identical bills were being offered by friendly congressmen in the House.

Ten years later, deregulation remained the core issue of Representative Lionel Van Deerlin's rewrite of the Communications Act of 1934, the big legislative news, so far as broadcasting was concerned, of 1978. The rewrite would have made deregulation a reality, "a bigger giveaway of public rights and property than Teapot Dome," according to Dr. Everett Parker, head of the Office of Communications of the United Church of Christ and the nation's most persistent proponent of public interest in broadcasting. Despite the excitement attendant upon the preparation and presentation of Van Deerlin's document, the rewrite, attacked by all interested parties for diverse reasons, was itself rewritten and then effectively shelved for the foreseeable future.

Deregulation, however, continued as an issue in Senate Communications Subcommittee legislation drafted by Senators Ernest Hollings and Barry Goldwater. In the FCC, a plan for the deregulation of radio had received a favorable response, based on the assumption that the large number of radio stations (grown from 6,276 in 1968 to over 8,600 in 1979) promised a diversity that over-the-air TV with its limited number of channels could not offer. Also, proponents claimed that many small-market radio stations were already doing far more public service broadcasting than suggested by FCC guidelines. Nevertheless, the overall impression of radio's direction in the past decade, with a few notable exceptions, seemed not toward improved quality but toward a suffocating uniformity, particularly on the FM band, which when it was opened up in 1941 was hailed as the last and best hope for quality broadcasting.*

All-news radio, the medium's most significant recent development so far as broadcast journalists were concerned, hit a high of 118 stations coast to coast in 1979 after surviving a major setback in 1977, when NBC's Radio News Information Service went under with a $10 million loss. The explanation for its failure was that it was too "national" in its orientation.

The best job of radio journalism at the end of the decade was being done by National Public Radio. For the past eight years it had been responsible for some of the most consistently intelligent and literate news and commentary on the air in its ninety-minute daily *All Things Considered.* It had also shown the greatest readiness to plug into important events as they were unfolding. In the 1978–79 season this included extensive live coverage of the House Assassinations Committee hearings, the Senate Foreign Relations Committee and

*On December 26, the United Church of Christ's Office of Communications filed a suit in Manhattan's Federal District Court in an attempt to prevent the FCC from deregulating the radio industry without letting the public know the basis for its decision. The suit maintained the FCC was withholding documents from the public —information that public interest groups would want in preparing their comments.

Armed Services Committee hearings on the SALT II treaty, House hearings on the DC-10, House and Senate hearings on Three Mile Island, and the hearings of the Presidential Commission on Three Mile Island. In the fall of 1979, NPR had added another full two-hour news and public affairs stretch five mornings a week, the direct result of a $4 million increase in its allotted budget from the Corporation for Public Broadcasting.

That National Public Radio, largely dependent on the government for its funds, was producing some of the frankest and most outspoken journalism of the day was a demonstration that even without the dropping of regulatory chains, controversial and critical material could get on the air.

In the 1960s, management was still able to claim that news and public affairs were the tribute broadcasting paid in return for certain regulatory protections and privileges. The logic behind this argument weakened as the success of broadcast journalism and its importance to the economic well-being of networks and individual stations became more and more apparent.

With broadcast journalism the primary news source for 67 percent of the nation and the only U.S. institution whose credibility actually increased rather than dwindled over the decade, the question was no longer whether it deserved full First Amendment protection. Given the peculiar nature of broadcasting, and journalism's position within the parent enterprises, the question was whether or not the First Amendment was protection *enough*.

Already in 1969, FCC Commissioner Nicholas Johnson had pointed out that in America's eleven largest cities there were no independent locally owned network-affiliated VHF stations. The impact of conglomerate ownership on the news and public affairs operations of the stations under their command had been the subject of an FCC inquiry begun in 1969 and abandoned in 1973.

Meanwhile, media monopolies and outside ownership were growing. In 1968, prolonged Justice Department litigation finally prevented the acquisition of the American Broadcasting Company by the International Telephone and Telegraph Corporation, ostensibly because of the possible compromising of journalistic standards such an association could cause. Since then, the possible negative effect of broadcast acquisitions by big business and the growing phenomenon of broadcasting itself acquiring substantial non-media properties were all but ignored. The FCC ruling against cross ownership of publishing and broadcasting properties in the same community, upheld by the Supreme Court, dealt only with a small portion of the possible conflicts of interest introduced by this growing corporate tangle.

Although provable instances of direct pressure on news operations from their endless list of corporate cousins and in-laws were few and far between—indeed, the supposed anti-business bias of the journalists was a recurring complaint throughout the decade—the possibility and the temptation were there. Furthermore, the diminishing segment that news operations represented in these sprawling enterprises also has to be considered. Given these facts, the threat to quality journalism from management intrusion or indifference seemed at least as great as that associated with government licensing and the lack of First Amendment guarantees.

Still, government continued to be seen as a present and potential danger, particularly in the apparent hostility toward the press evidenced by the Burger Court in such decisions as *Herbert* v. *Lando, Zurcher* v. *Stanford Daily,* and *Gannett* v. *DePasquale* (see the report by Tom Goldstein, "The Burger Court and Broadcasting: An Uneasy Balance," in Part III).

The ultimate test of how compatible a democratic government was with the information function of broadcasting no doubt lay in the health of news and public affairs on the Public Broadcasting Service. Here the government not only regulated but also appointed top executives and funded their activities. Public radio has already been cited as a heartening example of the compatibility of good news and government sponsorship. Unfortunately, the same cannot be said for public television, whose budget was seven times as large and whose audience was ten times as large.

At the beginning of the decade, public television was setting the pace for its commercial colleagues in terms of news commitment. In the season of 1968–69, there were more prime-time documentaries on public TV than on the three commercial networks combined. *The Public Broadcasting Laboratory* and *The Great American Dream Machine* were groundbreakers in the TV magazine field. Such series as *The Nader Reports* and *Behind the Lines* were taking television viewers into controversial areas that the other networks all too frequently neglected. And during the course of Watergate, it was public television that was most faithful and exhaustive in its coverage.

But by the time the impeachment hearings were adjourned and Nixon had taken off by helicopter from the White House lawn, public TV journalism had already gone into a serious decline. The Nixon team, which had tried to weaken the hegemony of the commercial networks through regulatory threats and other pressures and failed, had succeeded all too well with the more vulnerable Public Broadcasting Service, where Nixon appointees were firmly entrenched.

The cutting back and ultimate disappearance of NPACT (National Public Affairs Center for Television), the only TV entity to air the entire sequence of Watergate and impeachment hearings, was indicative of the process that had been set in motion. The new Station Program Cooperative, which purported to be a step toward democratizing public broadcasting by encouraging local production, had the effect of making it almost impossible for important documentaries to get on the air. A parallel development that delivered much of prime-time public network space up to big corporate funders, and the entertainment blockbusters they preferred, likewise militated against the development of controversial news and public affairs series. Although throughout the decade individual news programs and documentaries of distinction were aired, public broadcasting no longer had the edge over its commercial competition that it could claim at the opening of the decade.

The findings of the Carnegie Commission report, issued in the first month of 1979, gave some indication of the damage done and the concern that a highly respected panel of experts had for its repair. Among the observations:

> Journalism has been the greatest area of peril for public broadcasters. In the early 1970s, public broadcasting's outspoken public affairs presence prompted a powerful demand for conformity from the Nixon administration. Once burned, the sys-

tem, substantially financed by tax dollars, was less tempted to seek controversy or to perform a journalistic role that occasionally earns the displeasure of local pressure groups and government itself.

Yet, while it has a difficult course to chart, public broadcasting *must* develop a strong professional and independent public affairs presence if it is to be respected as an important public voice. Without becoming an agent of propaganda for any ideological position or any geographical elite and without setting itself up as an arbiter of taste or of cultural orthodoxy, public broadcasting must become a journalistic enterprise that calls events as it sees them.

There are some within public broadcasting who will actively resist this recommendation, preferring the blandness that raises no one's hackles. This is not the life of the serious artist or journalist. We certainly do not advocate that public broadcasters should be granted unlimited license to sensationalize or distort in order to titillate audiences, but rather that they be allowed to become a free institution that disciplines itself by constant comparison with truth.

. . . We believe, for example, that a mature journalistic role for public broadcasting will require that the institution speak out on matters of public policy, attempt to uncover wrongdoing, and occasionally criticize those in high places. Such criticism must be truthful and fair, but we believe that appropriate standards should be allowed to develop within the system, rather than by statute.

To bring this desirable state of affairs about, the commission recommended the funding of an op-ed page for TV and radio, the training of commentators, and the financing of units to produce mini-documentaries, documentaries, and magazine shows resembling those it once had pioneered and been forced to abandon.

Elsewhere, there were other gestures toward the rehabilitation of public TV news and public affairs. By the end of the decade, the Corporation for Public Broadcasting had set up a $1 million revolving fund for the sponsoring of documentaries from independent producers. Unfortunately, the first program funded, Don Widener's highly controversial "Plutonium: An Element of Risk," was rejected on journalistic grounds.

David Loxton's TV Laboratory was given grants totaling $500,000 to distribute to independent documentary producers. And ABC had indicated its friendliness by buying the award-winning "Police Tapes" and giving it national exposure when the public system had rejected it as too local in its interest. ABC also granted $50,000 and the use of its archives for a PBS series on Vietnam. The reorganization of the PBS system and CPB's establishment of an independent programming facility called the Program Fund with $27.5 million at its disposal could also have a benign effect.

But despite these encouraging signs there was an atmosphere of gloom that had to do with the failure of public television budgets to keep pace with the demands of inflation. Public TV managements feared they had reached the maximum of spontaneous public support, which would inevitably slack off when alternate technologies began providing the quality fare that had been one of public TV's principal raisons d'être. The growth of new technologies could likewise distract legislators' attention from the Public Broadcasting Service's growing needs.

Richard Wald, between his job as top news man at

NBC and joining Roone Arledge as News Vice President at ABC, undertook to study public broadcasting's journalism needs. In his "Possible Courses for News and Public Affairs," he recommended the expansion of the *MacNeil/Lehrer Report* to one hour every night, a fifty-two-week-a-year documentary series, and an ambitious weekend roundup. So far none of the suggestions seems close to realization.

Equally disheartening were the words of Bill Moyers, who had given up his cushy job at CBS to return to his first love, public TV, and who had the best deal given to an individual newsman by PBS to date. At the beginning of the second season of *Bill Moyers' Journal*, he delivered a sad commentary to a group of his colleagues in public broadcasting:

> I'm not at all optimistic, in fact, that public broadcasting is a home for journalists. There is very little reporting on public television. Mostly, we talk about the world, instead of capturing it on film and tape. *Wall Street Week* talks about the stock market. It does not show how it works. *Washington Week in Review* talks about the nation's capital. It does not show us what happens. *MacNeil/Lehrer* talks about the news. It does not report it. *Bill Moyers' Journal* at least half of the time relies on interviews with people talking about their lives, not capturing in biography the way they live or the ideas they hold.
>
> I yield to no one in my respect for the talking head. Talk separates us from the animals. But I also know the power of video and film to communicate more than words alone. And I believe that public broadcasting will never really matter until most of its journalism is in showing and experiencing instead of discussing and talking.

Part II:

The Hydra:
Technology Rampant

In 1979, two events—the accident at Three Mile Island and the fuel crisis that suddenly returned in May and promised to go on forever—vividly dramatized how far the double dilemma of environment and energy had deepened in one short decade.

No longer just a middle-class crusade for conservation and against pollution, it had become a tangle of issues that now intimidated and inconvenienced everyone and involved all aspects of Americans' daily lives— the food they ate, the cars they drove, the jobs they held, the pills they took, the machines and chemicals they relied on at home and on the job. The legendary know-how that Americans had so long and justifiably put their faith in fell to earth in the flaming heaps of Skylab and the DC-10, skidded to a deadly halt in the Ford Pinto on Firestone 400 radials. The depressing feeling that the entire biosphere was irretrievably despoiled dribbled and nibbled its way into the nation's consciousness with acid rain, asbestos fibers, PBB, DES, carcinogenic diet colas, Agent Orange, nitrites, vinyl chloride, and chemical wastes.

The energy-environment-technology story that broadcasters in the past ten years had made peculiarly their own was as difficult to handle as any that journalists had ever confronted. The political and economic stakes were astronomical, the social ramifications overwhelming, the technical issues incomprehensible. Experts brave enough to announce that they had arrived at the truth were as often as not challenged by other experts who announced the exact opposite. And corporate and governmental officials compounded the confusion with their anxious misrepresentations, cover-ups, and general inability to cope.

The broadcast journalist's task was to represent the interest of an increasingly bewildered American public, to ask the necessary questions, and to sort through and present fairly and simply the complex scientific, political, and moral choices to be made on energy and environmental issues. TV and radio met this formidable challenge with varying degrees of success.

8/A Big Bubble?

At precisely thirty-eight seconds after four o'clock on the quiet morning of Wednesday, March 28, 1979, a high-pitched whistle pierced the dark stillness of the peaceful Pennsylvania countryside thirteen miles southeast of Harrisburg. But the loud, shrill sound of steam escaping under high pressure—the result of a pump failure in the cooling system of the three-month-old nuclear power plant at nearby Three Mile Island—did not awaken most of the slumbering residents of the area. Indeed, what was to become the 1978–79 season's biggest and most difficult news story went unreported until long after dawn.

At 8:00 A.M. Dave Edwards ("Captain Dave"), a traffic reporter for Harrisburg radio station WKBO, heard over his CB radio that police and firefighters were mobilizing in Middletown. He notified WKBO's news director, Mike Pintek, who immediately called Three Mile Island to find out what was going on. Someone in the reactor's control room told him, "I can't talk now, we've got a problem," and referred him to Metropolitan Edison headquarters in Reading, Pennsylvania,

sixty miles away. There Pintek learned that a "general
emergency" had been declared at 7:24 A.M., but Met
Ed spokesman Blaine Fabian assured him that the public was in no danger. At 8:25, Pintek finally broke the
TMI story to the public. "I tried to tone it down so
people wouldn't be alarmed," he said. It was another
half hour before the first wire service dispatch was sent
out to newsrooms across the country. Echoing Met Ed's
own report to local authorities, it dismissed the event
at TMI as routine. "They said there's no radiation leak,"
one state trooper was quoted in the AP story. "Whatever it is, it's contained."

Had those two initial news reports been right, the
incident at Three Mile Island never would have made
it to the evening news. As it turned out, the events at
TMI's Unit 2 dominated network newscasts for the following "twelve days of terror" (in Walter Cronkite's
words) and snapped the nation out of its complacent
acceptance of the inevitability of nuclear power. For
broadcasters, Three Mile Island had all the ingredients
of other recent environmental stories—conflicting
facts, contradictory experts, corporate stonewalling,
and regulatory bungling and cover-up. And it had an
even more compelling element: the terrifying possibility that at each step of the unfolding sequence of events
catastrophe might be imminent.

In the first forty-eight hours, as Met Ed technicians
and scientists manipulated pumps and valves to bring
the soaring temperatures and radiation inside the reactor down to a stable, safe level, at least two hundred
reporters descended on the sparsely populated area
surrounding TMI. Three hundred more would arrive
before the week was over. While local radio stations
threw everybody on their shoestring staffs into the field

to help inform their frightened listeners, the TV networks mobilized small armies to gather the news for the rest of the world. NBC rushed in eight correspondents, two overall producers, six field producers, three coordinating producers, one equipment supervisor, an electronic news gathering (ENG) supervisor, three ENG editors, and two radiation experts. ABC in the first thirty-six hours sent in four correspondents, four field producers, four camera crews, and three editors. CBS's producer at the site, Jonathan Ward, was told by a network vice-president, "Anything you want, do it." He brought in three film crews, a second reporter from Washington, a second film editor, and a maintenance man to take care of the editing equipment. "After we brought in the Washington crews," Ward later told a presidential commission task force investigating Three Mile Island, "I wanted a Winnebago for a camera platform to be set up at the observation center. The Winnebago dealer in Middletown asked me, 'Will you buy it if it becomes radioactive?' New York said, 'No sweat.' "

Worried that their correspondents on the scene might be in physical danger from radiation, the networks rotated their reporters and took other precautions. ABC provided its staff with a medical team headed by a physician, throwaway protective suits, radiation meters, and a six-page evacuation plan that designated second and third fallback positions more than twenty miles away. NBC personnel wore film badges to measure radiation exposure, and CBS had a bus outfitted with protective suits for the staff in case of evacuation. Despite these precautions, several reporters and two network camera crews refused to go to TMI.

Those who agreed to take the chance ran up against one of the toughest assignments of their careers. Beyond the obvious physical risks, there were logistical problems. The rural TMI area simply wasn't set up to accommodate hundreds of out-of-town reporters and crews. Those who arrived the first day found Met Ed's press center locked, with a handwritten sign on the door saying, "For updates and further information call our main office in Reading." But finding a phone was no easy task. On Thursday, the second day of the crisis, two hundred reporters showed up at Met Ed's tour center across the Susquehanna River from TMI, complaining that there was only one phone in the area—and it was broken.

Even if a reporter could get to a phone in the first couple of days, he or she had to wait as much as four hours just to reach a media representative from the Nuclear Regulatory Commission in Bethesda, Maryland, the next source to which reporters resorted. It wasn't until the fifth day that a legitimate press center with phones, long tables, and an area for press conferences was set up in Middletown's Federal Hall. Ill-prepared and disorganized, the NRC staff did not provide mimeographed sheets with information on the reactor's condition and nuclear power in general until the sixth day.

During the first two days, most of the reporters' information about the accident came from Met Ed public relations staffers, who insisted that the public was in no danger. But as early as the afternoon of the first day, reporters had reason to be skeptical about the utility's pronouncements. After his meeting with Met Ed officials, Pennsylvania Lieutenant Governor William Scranton III told newsmen, "The situation is more complex than the company first led us to believe. Metropolitan Edison has given you and us conflicting information." Met Ed had admitted to Scranton that the uranium fuel core of the reactor had already been damaged—the first step on the way to the "impossible" meltdown evoked in the movie *The China Syndrome,* released just the month before.

Scranton's statement and other reports that radiation from the plant had been released and detected up to sixteen miles away were enough to put several local families to flight. The next day, Thursday, when Met Ed dumped more than 40,000 gallons of radioactive waste water into the Susquehanna River to make room for the overflow from the accident, Met Ed Vice-President Jack Herbein told reporters in nearby Middletown, "There is presently no danger to the public health or safety. We didn't injure anybody. We didn't overexpose anybody. And we certainly didn't kill anybody. The radiation off site was absolutely minuscule."

Although subsequent investigations have revealed that Met Ed officials suspected how serious the accident was and withheld the information from authorities for two days, at the time it was almost impossible to confirm or disprove the utility's version of events. Alton Slagle of the *New York Daily News* said later:

> One of the insidious things about TMI is that you couldn't see what they were fighting. You've got an invisible enemy. . . . It makes it particularly tough on television coverage because everything looked so deceptively innocent. . . . We eventually flew over the thing, looking down on it. There was no sign of anything being wrong. You can't see radiation. When you can't see radiation and you can't get good information you're in trouble, and that's what we were facing.

The TV networks knew at the outset that TMI was an important story. But because their reporters could not fully believe Met Ed and at the same time had no way to verify independently what was happening inside the reactor, their broadcasts in the first two days were restrained. All three network newscasts led with Three Mile Island on Wednesday night. They gave viewers the sense that a serious accident had taken place, but they chose their words carefully to avoid panic. ABC, for instance, decided not to use any adjective that had not been used by authorities. Only NBC mentioned that a general emergency had been declared. And Walter Cronkite's lead that Wednesday, more alarming than those of the other networks, was rewritten several times "to get the right tone":

> Good evening. It was the first step in a nuclear nightmare; as far as we know at this hour, no worse than that. But a government official said that a breakdown in an atomic power plant in Pennsylvania today is probably the worst nuclear accident to date. There was no serious contamination of workers. But a nuclear safety group said that radiation inside the plant is at eight times the deadly level; so strong that after passing through a three-foot-thick concrete wall, it can be measured a mile away.

The overall impression the networks conveyed that first night was that the radiation had been contained and that the worst seemed to be over. And the next night, according to the News Study Group at the Massachusetts Institute of Technology, "There was a general feeling of post-mortem in the newscasts; what remained was the complete cold shutdown of the reactor, an extensive cleanup and—the thrust of the story now —long investigation to find out what had happened."

Everything changed, though, when on Friday two strong uncontrolled bursts of radiation broke loose from the plant. Instead of packing their bags, the newspeople brought in reinforcements and expanded their coverage to Washington. There the story was just beginning. The five-member Nuclear Regulatory Commission, regulator of all seventy-two nuclear power plants in the country, convened a day-long session at 9:00 A.M. to deal with the events at TMI. Tapes of that meeting revealed a frightening confusion and inability to get accurate information at the highest levels. Harold Denton, director of the NRC's Office of Nuclear Reactor Regulation, reported to NRC Chairman Joseph Hendrie that he was having trouble with Met Ed. "It is really difficult to get the data," Denton said. "We seem to get it after the fact. They opened the valves this morning for the letdown, and were releasing [radiation] at a six curie per second rate before anyone knew about it."

NRC's information chief, Joseph Fouchard, called from Harrisburg during the meeting to report that Pennsylvania Governor Richard Thornburgh had complained of "ambiguous" information from the plant. A mid-level NRC official in Pennsylvania had advised Thornburgh to evacuate the TMI area, but Thornburgh wanted a recommendation from Hendrie himself. Hendrie told Fouchard, "His [Thornburgh's] information is ambiguous, mine is nonexistent, and—I don't know— it's like a couple of blind men staggering around making decisions."

If the chairman of the NRC and the governor of Pennsylvania were having trouble getting reliable information, the problem was more devastating for the broadcasters. Even if they managed to overcome their logistical difficulties, reporters still had to contend with the most disturbing problem of all: whom to believe. Their sources were limited to the NRC on the scene, the NRC in Washington, the governor's office, Met Ed, and any outside experts they could dig up. And they all seemed to be saying different things, a phenomenon that Governor Thornburgh later dubbed the "garble gap." Tom Wolzien, one of NBC's two overall producers, told *Broadcasting* magazine, "I've never been on anything [like this story, where] you've mistrusted every bit of information."

Reporters, the governor, and the NRC charged that Met Ed was evading the truth by saying that everything was safe and under control. Met Ed President Walter Creitz denied cover-up charges but later admitted to the *Reading Eagle* that the company "should have been more pessimistic." On the other hand, Met Ed public relations director Blaine Fabian explained to the *Columbia Journalism Review* that "it wasn't like a train wreck—the facts kept changing from moment to moment. Reporters didn't seem to understand that."*

Indeed, some reporters were indignant that they were getting contradictory statements even from NRC officials. The awful truth was that no one—not outside experts, not government officials, not Met Ed—actually

*Malcolm Browne of *The New York Times*, at a Sigma Delta Chi panel discussion in June, put himself in Met Ed's position: "Now, being a devil's advocate for a moment, I would also say that a spokesman, however well-intentioned and well-qualified, when confronted with . . . a maelstrom of people with questions—when are we going to die? when are you going to evacuate us? and so forth —that it would be impossible to answer a question in any reasonable way."

knew for sure what was happening. Because of the radiation, no one could get inside the reactor to see, and officials even doubted the accuracy of the readings they were getting from instruments that had been exposed to constant radiation and temperatures up to 4,000 degrees Fahrenheit.

Late Friday morning, Governor Thornburgh advised all persons living within ten miles of TMI to stay indoors with all windows and doors shut until the new releases of radiation could be measured. At 12:30 P.M. the governor urged pregnant women and preschool children living within five miles of the plant to evacuate. When confused reporters asked Met Ed spokesman Jack Herbein why such actions were necessary, he could only answer, "We have our windows and doors open."

Dispatched by helicopter at President Carter's orders, NRC's Harold Denton arrived at TMI at 2:00 P.M. Friday with a dozen nuclear scientists. He realized immediately that Met Ed did not have the technical ability to handle the accident. Matters were more complicated and dangerous than anyone had imagined. There was, or so it seemed to the NRC, a hydrogen bubble growing within the reactor. It had the potential to explode, destroy the four-foot-thick concrete walls, and release all the pent-up radiation from the accident upon the peaceful countryside. While Denton described the possibility of a meltdown as "very remote," it was still real enough to 100,000 people in the area that they got into their cars and headed for the nearest Interstate, leaving Middletown, Goldsboro, and other neighboring villages looking like abandoned movie sets.

The networks responded lavishly to all the revelations and unanswered questions of that dramatic Friday, devoting more than half their evening newscasts to Three Mile Island. Later that night, CBS aired a one-hour special report giving the matter some perspective and background, while ABC and NBC each offered a half hour. "In terms of information," said John Chancellor, reflecting the views of most reporters, "this thing is a mess."

The White House apparently agreed with Chancellor's assessment and decided that communications needed to be centralized. Ignoring Met Ed, it designated Governor Thornburgh as the sole source of news on evacuation matters and Harold Denton as the sole source of information at the reactor site. "Well, I think we know what we are doing," Denton told reporters, "but we have never had such extensive fuel damage in the life of any reactor."

When Denton became the spokesman for the NRC, the mouths of other NRC officials seemed to close, making the job of the newsman even more difficult. The Friday afternoon tapes of the NRC's meeting reveal that Chairman Hendrie talked to Presidential Press Secretary Jody Powell about how to handle the PR aspect of the accident. Powell's advice, apparently, was to say nothing. NRC Commissioner Richard Kennedy had been invited to appear on *Meet the Press* that Sunday, but when Hendrie, acting on the advice of Powell, told him to cancel out, Kennedy replied, "That's eminently sensible." And NRC Commissioner Victor Gilinsky was convinced by the White House to cancel his appearance on the *MacNeil-Lehrer Report* at the last minute. Commissioner Kennedy's comment: "Tough, the life of a newsman. That's why they drink so much. They're always losing their stories just before they file them."

Chairman Hendrie apparently did not share Commissioner Kennedy's sympathy for the newsman's plight. Later in the tapes he is heard to say, as he puzzles over how to deal with the media, "Which amendment is it that guarantees freedom of the press? Well, I'm against it."

On Saturday, with Met Ed's Herbein maintaining that "the crisis is over," Denton began directing efforts to remove the volatile hydrogen bubble. That night AP sent out an alarming advisory to all TV and radio stations: "The NRC now says the gas bubble atop the nuclear reactor at Three Mile Island shows signs of becoming potentially explosive." The information had come from an NRC source who claimed that the attempt to reduce the hydrogen bubble could possibly cause a meltdown within a few days. At a late-night news conference, Denton confirmed the possibility of a meltdown or a hydrogen explosion. Estimating that neither could happen for at least twelve days, he assured reporters that he intended to eliminate the bubble before then.

Like so much else at TMI, the hydrogen bubble was not an easy concept for a reporter to grasp, let alone translate into plain English for the public. Few of the reporters on the scene had technical training or previous experience reporting on science or energy. Those who had were still at a loss. "Unless you were a nuclear scientist," ABC energy specialist Roger Peterson said, "you didn't know what on earth was going on."

All three networks hired nuclear experts to help their reporters sift through the complex technical questions. ABC had nuclear physicist Mort Heller. CBS had Long Island radiologist Harry Astarita (nicknamed "Radiation Harry" by other reporters) on the scene, and George Rathjens, a nuclear specialist working for the Carter administration, was available for phone consultation. NBC had University of Pennsylvania radiologist James Brennan and John Davis of the consulting firm of Radiation Management Corporation, as well as Dr. Herbert Koutz of the Brookhaven National Laboratory on Long Island.

Broadcasters found that one way to avoid the technical mumbo jumbo was to focus on the human-interest side of the story. For citizens who got their information about TMI only by watching TV, what the guy on the street feared was happening inside the reactor became just as important as what actually was happening.

On Sunday morning, the fifth day, President Carter arrived by helicopter, donned yellow boots for the TV cameras, and toured the plant. Meanwhile, the news media were told that the hydrogen bubble that had mysteriously appeared had now just as mysteriously begun to shrink. By Monday at 9:45 A.M., Met Ed spokesman George Troffer announced, "The bubble is gone. The reactor is completely stable and ready for final cooldown. There are no problems left. We are not emitting any radioactive gases." At 11:15, Denton pretty much confirmed Troffer's statement—one of the few times during the crisis that the NRC and Met Ed had agreed on anything. Several days later, Denton felt the situation was safe enough to admit, "Time is on our side." In another week, the pregnant women and small children returned, and the crisis was indeed over.

No fewer than six state and federal investigations of what had happened at TMI got under way almost immediately. The most important of these was a special twelve-member presidential commission chaired by Dartmouth College President John Kemeny.* (See the report by commission member Carolyn Lewis, "Three Mile Island," in Part III.) Part of the commission's mandate was to find out whether the public's right to information was well served during the emergency. A task force was assigned by the commission to focus specifically on the performance of public-information officials and the news media. After six months, the commission included the task force's conclusions in its report to the President. "A combination of confusion and weakness in the sources of information and lack of understanding on the part of the media resulted in the public being poorly served," wrote the commission. It recommended that federal and state agencies and utility companies prepare a "systematic public information program" for emergencies that would include press centers close to the site. "These must be properly equipped," the commission said, "have appropriate visual aids and reference materials, and be staffed with individuals who are knowledgeable in dealing with the news media." It went on to recommend that the news media train specialists to report on nuclear matters, learn to place complex information in a context that is understandable to the public, and "educate themselves

*The Kemeny commission appointed two advisory committees of its own, one representing the energy industry and the other representing American citizens. The citizens' panel, picked by Reverend William Millard, a Jesuit priest and physicist who directed the Washington-based Interfaith Coalition of Energy, was disbanded at the end of July. The reason: the nine members, all of whom were skeptical about nuclear energy, wanted access to all commission documents and an advance look at the final report. For the sake of fairness, the commission dismissed the industry panel at the same time.

to understand the pitfalls in interpreting answers to 'what if' questions."

The Kemeny commission could not fault the broadcasters for skimping on resources, staff, and time poured into the TMI story. On the contrary, it called TMI "one of the most heavily covered media events ever" and concluded that "the extent of the coverage was justified." The importance of local radio as a source of information for local residents was considered paramount. Fifty-six percent of those responding to a survey made by Dr. Stanley Brunn of Michigan State University said that they first heard of the accident through local radio, and 62 percent cited radio as their "most frequent source of news" throughout the crisis. Most local radio stations changed their formats completely and increased their news coverage by 400 percent during the first week of the crisis. To handle the load, at least one station, WCMB Radio, Harrisburg, enlisted the services of salespeople and announcers and sent them out as reporters.

Local TV stations drastically modified their schedules as well. WHP Harrisburg ran three half-hour specials during the crisis. WTPA Harrisburg stayed on the air all night to cover breaking events both Friday and Saturday nights, March 30 and 31, and WGAL Lancaster did the same on Friday.

The three TV networks devoted a total of ten hours and nineteen minutes to TMI in morning and evening news shows and specials during the week of March 28–April 3. CBS and NBC gave an average of eleven minutes a night to TMI on their evening newscasts, and ABC averaged seven minutes. And the major news providers for radio stations outside the area had ample coverage as well. According to *Broadcasting* magazine:

The Mutual Broadcasting System, for example, had 50 cuts from its correspondent on the scene from just the first three days of coverage, not to mention later reporting. AP Radio claimed an all-time record for cuts Friday with 267 on Three Mile Island and other news of the day; the 5:30 A.M. to 1 A.M. cycle usually has 160–200. UPI Audio, with three audio staffers on the scene and reports from elsewhere, had several three-and-a-half-minute specials and was scheduling a 30-minute wrap-up last Friday [April 6].

Once the crisis was over, another source of contention long familiar to broadcasters was exposed: just what impact their massive presence and coverage had had on the situation at TMI. As the primary and most up-to-the-minute source of information for the population, broadcasters were in a particularly rough spot. They had to tread the fine line between portraying the accident as a catastrophe and thus throwing the local population into a panic, and lulling people into thinking things were okay when in fact they weren't. The task was doubly difficult since no one really knew at the time whether the wisest thing for locals to do was sit tight or pack up and leave. Steve Liddick, news director of WCMB Radio, Harrisburg, described the situation this way:

> Met Ed was saying everything is fine—routine. NRC people were saying there was a problem. Civil Defense was saying it was on alert. A siren would accidentally activate or someone would panic. People were terrified. They would reach for any scrap of information and then be afraid to believe it. We very easily could have stampeded the public.

In some instances, broadcasters held back information. Ed Wickenheiser, news director of WSBA Radio, York, knew about the emergency at TMI before 7:30 A.M. on Wednesday because his station was the primary Emergency Broadcast System station for the county. Though he had the story an hour before any other station, he chose not to put it on the air. Similarly, news director Mike Pintek of WKBO Harrisburg couldn't decide whether to air a recommendation by University of Pittsburgh Professor of Radiology Ernest Sternglass that pregnant women and preschool children should evacuate on Thursday, a day before the governor's order. The station used the report but withdrew it when it set off a panic in the area. Later Pintek put the story back on the air. "I realized that the public has a right to know all sides" he said later, "and a right to protect their own health."

At the time, the broadcasters were ambivalent, and some of them even wondered aloud about their proper role. Walter Cronkite, on CBS's one-hour special two days after the accident, found himself addressing an essentially introspective question to nuclear proponent Ralph Lapp:

> CRONKITE: [Dr. Lapp] mentioned a moment ago that we've in the last two years been going through a sort of radiation hysteria. Does he feel that reports such as this tonight are adding to that hysteria? Or what does he feel the public should be told about an incident such as this we're undergoing now?
>
> LAPP: In referring, Walter, to the matter of radiation hysteria, I am referring to the reports that have been publicized, largely by the media and certainly by the electronic media, on the effects of

low-level radiation. I'm not indicting this program. In fact, Walter, I would congratulate you. I think, given the time required, you did a good wrap-up on this. I enjoyed the presentation. I'm not quarreling with—

CRONKITE: I didn't ask the question only as a matter of personal pride. [Laughs] I—

LAPP: No, No. I—

CRONKITE: I was asking it because it's a serious matter of public information in these things.

In the months after the accident, Cronkite's question was answered by numerous media critics and interested parties. Their most fervent complaint was that the broadcasters had sensationalized the events at TMI. Dr. Lapp, who runs a nuclear consulting business called Quadri-Science, Inc., wrote to *The New York Times,* "Make no mistake about it, TMI-2 was a bad accident, but it was overplayed as a media event. The NRC propagated a 'hydrogen bubble' threat when in fact there was none."* Met Ed, which took the most knocks from the press during the crisis for providing totally unreliable information, predictably agreed with Lapp. Its newly hired PR agency, the giant Hill & Knowlton, told *Advertising Age,* "We feel the furor over nuclear power is not entirely justified, and reports made by scientists have proved that the press blew this thing way out of proportion. The press was playing with the public's fear of the unknown."

The proof of media sensationalism, wrote engineer

---

*Dr. Roger Mattston of the NRC, testifying later, confirmed Lapp's view that there was no real threat from a hydrogen bubble. At the time, the NRC's readings of faulty instruments led it to believe that the bubble did exist and was a real threat. Broadcasters passed this judgment on to the public.

Myron Kayton on *The New York Times* op-ed page, lay in the outcome of TMI:

> It is becoming apparent that nothing really happened at TMI to endanger the public, except in the fevered minds of some journalists. No employees were hurt or killed, nor was any citizen injured. So far as I have read, the only damage seems to have been the release of a small amount of slightly radioactive water from the nuclear plant. Despite a wildly improbable sequence of human errors, the plant's safety systems worked and the public was protected.
>
> . . . Why all the furor? Newsmen were asking plant engineers: "Could meltdown occur?" "Could the hydrogen bubble explode?" Being good engineers, they said "yes," but were interrupted before they could explain that the probability of these catastrophes was remote. Yet fanned by the rage of ideologically antinuclear groups, by conservative groups opposed to change, and by the coincidental release of the film "The China Syndrome," the public was led to believe that nuclear power is spectacularly unsafe.

In his *Newsweek* column George Will, a proponent of nuclear power, took a poke at an unnamed network's sloppy use of language: "After the hydrogen bubble began dissolving, one network still referred to the Harrisburg 'calamity.' What language does that network reserve for events that kill people?" And President Carter, who had himself helped repair a damaged nuclear reactor in the 1950s, was reported by Evans and Novak to have called some of the TMI reporting "exaggerated," "irresponsible," and "outrageous."

The networks even took some potshots from the local stations that covered TMI. Charles Smith, president and general manager of radio station WPDC in Elizabethtown, seven miles from the reactor, said, "The local media has a much better slant on it than the national media, especially national TV. The outside representatives are about the rudest bunch of people I think I've ever seen. They've tried to put words into the mouths of spokesmen that are downright inflammatory."

WHP Harrisburg news director Herb Thurman added, "We found our reports varying greatly from the network reports at the time. The nets were frequently talking about the possibility of the ultimate disaster with fifty-five or sixty thousand people killed. It's nice to report something like that from afar. But it was a little irresponsible as far as local use goes."

But there were those who defended the media and gave the newspeople credit for serving the public well. Most prominent and closest to the accident was Governor Richard Thornburgh, who during the crisis had his differences with the press. Nearly a month after the accident, though, he told the NRC:

> [There were] many moments when reporters did a better job of putting events into perspective than did the officials who were shaping those events. . . .
>
> If some press accounts were an occasional threat to those who might panic, most were a continuing check on those who might deceive. Their place in this emergency was indispensable.

The New York Times's Tom Wicker noted that the nuclear industry and its apologists had launched a counterattack against the media, trying to blame reporters for TMI:

> The effort to shift the burden of guilt to the press is as familiar as Spiro Agnew used to be. Granted that newspapers and broadcasters have many sins to answer for; granted, too, that the press does not have its own authorities on nuclear physics, or many reporters with a solid knowledge of that field.
>
> Here again it was the potential of the thing that demanded coverage as urgent and extensive as a press so limited could provide. And here again it was the confusion and obfuscation and misleading statements of officials presumed to be knowledgeable and responsible that were principally responsible for confused and occasionally overwrought coverage. It ill becomes those whose failures and errors threatened such catastrophe to point a finger at reporters whose duty was to inform the public as best they could.
>
> Nor should it be forgotten that those who used to say it couldn't happen are now those who say nothing really did happen. No thanks to them, the public knows better on both counts.

The truth about the broadcasters' handling of TMI probably lay somewhere in between the attacks of the nuclear proponents and the defense of the nuclear skeptics. The MIT News Study Group, examining specifically television's coverage of the accident, concluded:

> Television news moved with admirable responsibility initially, even to the point of being slow with the story. Television news reported carefully both industry and government accounts from

within the plant, though with a growing suspicion that the full story was not told. Television news eventually proved to be unprepared or unwilling to put together the specialized analysis and detailed explanation needed to clarify the whole story; at times, in fact, it avoided promising—but risky—reporting leads in favor of more conventional—and safer—coverage.

The Kemeny commission's task force on the public's right to information did a content analysis of media coverage and noted, "While the media can be criticized for missing some stories and failing to provide a context for others, they were generally not guilty of the most common criticism leveled at them: that they presented an overwhelmingly alarming view of the accident." This task force produced a table showing that ABC, CBS, and NBC had together broadcast 179 reassuring statements during the first week of the accident (59 percent) and only 123 alarming statements (41 percent).

The ultimate judge, of course, was the public. According to a *New York Times*/CBS poll, 96 percent of those interviewed said they had heard or read about the accident at TMI. Most did not fault the media for sensationalism. On the contrary, 55 percent thought the danger to the public at TMI was greater than they had been told, while only 8 percent believed the situation was less dangerous than it was portrayed. Only 20 percent believed that "public officials had been honest in telling the public all they knew about the danger from the accident." But the media got considerably higher marks: 60 percent thought that newspapers and TV had covered TMI fairly, while only 30 percent felt that the media had been unfair.

Broadcasters' coverage of TMI did not end with the immediate crisis. Reporters returned periodically to the scene to see how the cleanup of the plant was progressing and to talk with residents about the toll the accident had taken on their lives. Months later, many of the townspeople were still frightened, depressed, and angry. "Most people do not understand the psychological damage that has been done to residents within the five-mile radius surrounding the plant," said the area's Republican Congressman William Goodling. "Many have indicated that the peace of mind and quality of life which were so abundant in this area prior to the accident have disappeared. They believe that in the past they have been lied to or strongly misled in relationship to the safety aspects of nuclear power."

Two weeks after the accident, a pregnant resident who had just returned to her home with her young child told ABC's Bettina Gregory:

> I was scared, I really was. I was scared to the point where I sat up for five nights and cried myself to sleep. It was unbelievable . . . to deal with a child that could be born with any type of birth defect. [The child cries.] It's really rough . . . it really is.

The long-term effect of the radiation that had leaked at TMI was covered extensively, if inconclusively, by TV and radio. Radiation levels, it seemed, were nearly twice as high as the first estimates and were expected to rise further. TV viewers watched Secretary of Health, Education, and Welfare Joseph Califano at first claim that no cancer deaths would result from TMI, then later revise his prognosis to one to ten. On the other hand, Ralph Nader, in a clamorous debate filmed

by KCTS-TV in Hanford, Washington (a center for nuclear manufacture and the storage of nuclear wastes),
maintained that no one, including his opponent, the
peripatetic Ralph Lapp, could minimize the long-term
effects of radiation exposure:

> I recall in 1902, you know, the allowable dose for
> radiation was 900 times what it is now. In 1952 it
> was about 300 times. How can you make these
> statements [that no one will be harmed] knowing
> that, almost now by the year, the allowable-dose-
> of-radiation recommendation is reduced consis-
> tently?

The broadcasters' follow-up efforts ranged far beyond TMI. The accident, it became clear, had again
raised all the doubts that had lain dormant for years as
the nation's commitment to nuclear energy had expanded. In the months following TMI, it fell to the
broadcasters to untangle for a confused public the
bewildering web of scientific, medical, political, economic, and psychological questions surrounding the future of nuclear energy itself. Were nuclear plants safely
designed? Did their technical staffs receive adequate
training? Did the states provide workable evacuation
plans in case of emergency? How many would be killed
and injured in a worst-possible-case accident? Who
would pay for the damages—government, insurers,
utility, or consumer? And would banks be willing to
lend money to build new nuclear installations?

Touching on many of these questions, CBS aired a
one-hour prime-time program, "Fallout from Three
Mile Island," a month after the accident. PBS followed
two weeks later with an hour called "The Three Mile
Island Syndrome" and added another hour in the fall

with the more personal "The People of Three Mile Island." The other two networks confined their reports to spots on their newscasts, mainly following the progress of the various panels investigating TMI and its aftermath. On the local-station level, 71 percent of the news directors responding to the DuPont-Columbia Survey said that they had already covered the subject of nuclear energy before Three Mile Island, but 75 percent said that they had explored the problem again in relation to their own communities as a result of the accident.

Broadcasters polled the public, which had once been fairly unified in its approval of nuclear power, and found that it was growing more skeptical and divided on the issue. Whereas in 1977, 69 percent had approved of building new nuclear plants and only 21 percent had disapproved, after TMI a *New York Times* / CBS poll showed that approval had dropped to 46 percent while disapproval had climbed to 41 percent. And after TMI the number of people who favored building a nuclear plant in their own community (38 percent) dropped for the first time below those who were against a plant in their own community (56 percent).

Giving more time to the growing anti-nuclear protests than they had in previous years (PBS offered three hours live from Washington on May 6), broadcasters invited anti-nuclear guests to be on their talk shows and in some cases subjected themselves to pressure from sponsors who had a stake in future nuclear construction. For example, shortly before the accident at Three Mile Island, Jane Fonda appeared on a Barbara Walters special on ABC to talk about her controversial film *The China Syndrome* and its anti-nuclear message. General

Electric, one of the four biggest builders of nuclear reactors in the world, promptly withdrew its sponsorship of the show.*

Westinghouse Broadcasting, as a subsidiary of Westinghouse Electric Corporation, builder of thirty-eight nuclear reactors in operation in 1979 and of seventy-one more in various stages of development, was an even more clear-cut example of possible conflicts of interest. Between 1975 and August 1979, Westinghouse's WBZ-TV and Radio in Boston aired fifteen editorials favoring nuclear power. Only the first one pointed out that WBZ was owned by Westinghouse Electric, though even it did not mention the company's involvement in nuclear construction. Three months after the accident at Three Mile Island, WBZ editorialized that "nuclear power may not be loved. But for now we think it's essential." And Westinghouse's WJZ-TV in Baltimore took the same position, calling for tighter safety precautions and government supervision and noting, "We cannot and should not close our eyes to the possibilities of nuclear energy." On the other hand, Westinghouse's KYW-TV and Radio in Philadelphia, which had produced an impressive documentary, "Three Mile Island: Seven Days of Fear," demanded answers by "the authorities" to long-standing questions about nuclear energy, as well as a congressional investigation and tighter controls at nuclear plants.

After the TMI accident, nuclear builders, utility companies, and pro-nuclear organizations continued to use

*G.E.'s ABC affiliate, WNGE Nashville, however, carried the interview, as did WSOC Charlotte, North Carolina, the ABC affiliate of Cox Broadcasting, which was in line for a merger with the broadcasting and cable TV business of General Electric.

the airwaves to get the pro-nuclear message across. They formed an umbrella group called the Committee on Energy Awareness, which put forth a million-dollar media campaign, including a series of two- and three-minute radio interviews and public service announcements on both radio and TV. The American Nuclear Society, for its part, distributed to radio stations a dozen free ten-minute interviews with nuclear scientists. The utility companies, which had been pushing nuclear energy in TV and radio ads for a long time, financed a major study of TMI themselves and also began beefing up their PR staffs and training their executives for TV appearances. But in July they suffered a major setback when the FCC ruled that four California radio stations had violated the Fairness Doctrine by refusing anti-nuclear spots after running pro-nuclear ads. Environmental groups in northern California promptly came up with anti-nuclear TV spots to counter Pacific Gas & Electric's ads, which had been aired the previous fall. Five California stations agreed to air the ads, and Washington's Media Access Project said it would attempt to place the spots in other states where stations had carried utility company ads promoting nuclear power.

Many utilities realized after TMI, though, that advertising alone would not be enough to restore the public's confidence in their industry. One positive aftereffect of TMI, according to several news directors responding to the Survey, was that the attitudes of utility companies toward reporters changed considerably. For the first time, TV cameras were allowed into many nuclear plants. "TMI resulted in more cooperation from the local utility than we had ever encountered in the past," wrote a news director from Miami. "It even allowed an extensive tour of the local nuclear plant." A news director from Denver added, "The local utility company was most cooperative in the wake of TMI, so our coverage of nuclear power in Colorado was facilitated considerably." And from Moline, Illinois: "The nukes were extra careful to make themselves available after they saw the PR debacle at TMI. . . . We were allowed a complete tour of the nuclear generating station, and the issues on both sides were more than adequately covered."

Yet despite some utilities' change of heart, the survey disclosed that many of the same problems that reporters faced at TMI—uncooperative utility companies, confused federal bureaucracies, corporate secrecy, outright lies—persisted. "We were denied access to the nuclear plant when the public service commissioner toured the facility," complained a news director in Savannah. "We have never been granted access to the plant." A radio news director in Cedar Rapids, Iowa, wrote, "The nuclear plant in our community was shut down eight months due to cracks in cooling water pipes. We received almost no information from the utility unless we forced their hand by first contacting the federal Nuclear Regulatory Commission regional office in Chicago."

A station in Cortland, New York, ran into an obstacle course trying to follow up a local angle on TMI:

> A local firm supplied some materials to the TMI nuclear power plant. We discovered this fact and tried to find out the details. The firm countered our every move by calling ahead to contractors [and] other firms engaged in similar manufacturing processes and by contacting NRC. We got the story, but the company declared it wanted nothing further to do with us. We discovered, as did Pennsylvania officials, that the NRC is a mass of conflict-

ing information managed by people who don't know what the fellow at the next desk is saying or doing.

From Knoxville, Tennessee:

> The Tennessee Valley Authority, which controls all electric power and its generation in this area, put a lid on information on nuclear power about two weeks after TMI. We had planned to do a series on TVA's stand on nuclear power after TMI. If the ban on information had not been lifted when it was, we quite possibly would not have had that series.

From Rock Island, Illinois:

> We had a local incident in which a hydrogen gas leak near the Cordova nuclear plant caught fire, causing a scramble of emergency vehicles. The fire was on the nuclear plant property. Calls by our station to the public information office of Iowa-Illinois Gas & Electric brought a response that the fire was nothing more than a roofing material fire on a building some distance from the plant . . . and that there was no reason for concern. In fact, the story was totally fabricated, the fire was potentially serious, did cause a great deal of concern to fire officials, and had nothing to do with roofing material.

Many news directors called the nuclear story the toughest they'd ever tried to cover, and just as many admitted their own ignorance made it tougher. "We have made a strong effort to educate a couple of our reporters to expertise in the nuclear field," wrote a news director in Charlotte, North Carolina. "But still they are not physicists or engineers. And these are very complex questions. Knowing what is true is our toughest problem in covering the nuclear controversy."

Other news directors were discouraged by their inability to communicate nuclear information clearly to the public. "Making viewers understand how nuclear reactors work was difficult," said one news director from Urbana, Illinois. "Helping them understand what nuclear contamination was all about was impossible. Cutting through emotionalism was our goal, and we didn't really attain it." A Greenville, South Carolina, news director added, "The whole debate is so complex and so multifaceted that it has become mind-boggling for the layman—and often for the reporter writing the story."

Yet, as a rule, news directors were more optimistic. The coverage of TMI and their own follow-ups afterward, they thought, had heightened public awareness about nuclear issues. The incident had forced broadcasters to change their own attitudes and investigate with renewed persistence an issue that had been considered dull and better left to public officials. Those officials were forced to change their attitudes too. As a Seattle news director pointed out, "There remains a residual carry-over from the days of the AEC which seemed to reflect the attitude of 'don't worry about it, we know what we're doing and you wouldn't understand it anyway.' That won't wash any more—and it never should have."

9/Return of the Crunch

On Sunday, May 6, 1979, the same day that public TV carried its three-hour coverage of 100,000 anti-nuclear demonstrators marching on the Capitol in Washington, the streets and freeways of Los Angeles, normally jammed with cars, were eerily quiet. Traffic was unseasonably light, and the entrances to most gas stations were blocked with spare tires. At the few stations with gas to serve, cars were lined up for several blocks, their drivers somberly inching the vehicles forward with shoulder power. There, in the city that embodied the automobile age, the gas crisis had returned.

Whereas many Americans had dismissed Three Mile Island as a freak one-time occurrence thousands of miles from their homes, no one could ignore the gas problem. The empty pumps, the skyrocketing prices, the closed service stations, the odd-even rationing, and the inevitable gas lines had rapidly spread from southern California eastward.

The gas crunch was the biggest local story of the year,

and the local broadcasters responded with countless daily reports. Their TV cameras captured better than any print journalist could the anger and bewilderment, the boredom and the irritation, the frustration, the fear, and the desperation of normally comfortable Americans having to cope with an unwelcome, recurring reality. Local radio news was unmatched in its ability to broadcast up-to-the-minute information about when and where gas was available and at what price. And both local radio and TV slotted time for gas-saving tips.*

But local coverage had its limits. After the friendly advice had been doled out and glimpses of gas-line tantrums had faded into commercials, big questions loomed, the most persistent being: "Is the fuel crisis real?" Although 50 percent of those surveyed in a *New York Times*/CBS poll in July 1979 said they had changed their driving habits as a result of the gas shortage, a staggering 62 percent still did not believe that any real shortage existed.

For broadcasters, getting at the truth behind the energy crisis was one of the most important and frustrating assignments of the decade. "Insofar as it is an issue with lasting, pervasive impact on the United States," Robert Hanfling, executive assistant to the Deputy Secretary of Energy, told a meeting of AP broadcasters, "the reporting of the energy situation presents, and will continue to present, the greatest challenge to the press since the civil rights movement."

---

*ABC Radio Network, every day from May 16 to June 29, sent four two-minute spots to its 1,600 affiliates, providing practical advice on how to survive in a new era of energy limits.

No story had been covered more persistently and at greater length by broadcast journalists. In the five years since the last crisis, NBC had aired one three-hour documentary, a two-part two-hour special, a one-hour report, and a half-hour special on the subject. CBS had contributed a three-hour special of its own, plus four hour-long reports and eleven half-hours. Since 1976, PBS had added thirty-three programs devoted to oil, including three special reports. And in 1978–79 alone, ABC had aired two half-hour specials and one fifteen-minute report.

As for radio, National Public Radio had put on an impressive thirty-three hours of live congressional hearings, a thirteen-part series, and specials on oil totaling more than 130 hours. In 1978–79, CBS Radio had done two weekend series—one twenty-six parts, the other twenty-eight parts—and ABC Radio had distributed four twenty-part series to its affiliates. Energy Secretary James Schlesinger's testimony before a congressional committee on how the revolution in Iran would affect the American oil future, aired by CBS Radio in February 1979, was one of the few examples of live coverage from the capital by the commercial networks during the year.

All the TV and radio networks had aired hundreds of items on evening newscasts, and all had quizzed public officials and oil company executives on public affairs interview programs. And yet, despite all their efforts, broadcasters had largely failed to explain the whys of the crisis—why the gas pumps were dry, why the oil companies were making so much money, why the country still had no comprehensive energy policy. The public watched the tube and became progressively more divided, confused, and angry.

Robert Hanfling accounted for the broadcasters' failure and the public's lack of understanding simply enough:

> The need to file daily stories on energy, a hot topic since the onset of the Iranian revolution, has led too many media outlets to concentrate on superficial developments, like the price of gasoline at the pump . . . and has left too little time to dig down to the real stories underneath.

But news directors who answered this year's Alfred I. duPont-Columbia Survey said that when they did try to get below the surface of the oil situation they invariably got stuck in a quagmire of lies, cover-ups, inefficiency, ignorance, and contradictions—not the least of which came from Hanfling's own Energy Department. A few of their comments:

> The Energy Department was not able to tell us their figures. They rely on the major oil companies to report. But government doesn't stick the tanks. The skeptical public wants to know, and can you trust an oil company?
>
> *Seattle, Washington*

> We found it virtually impossible to explain to our viewers who was responsible for the oil shortage once the gas lines formed in California. We were able to touch on why through the use of extensive research and graphics. But we found the story too big, too international, for a local station. We did not have the resources to get inside government, OPEC, and the oil industry. I don't even feel the networks have been able to unravel the contradictions.
>
> *San Francisco, California*

> Large oil companies seem to have at least one person specializing in misleading reporters or

thinking up clever responses that never seem to answer questions.

Springfield, Illinois

During the current gas crunch, we contacted Exxon in Houston, only to find that they were not talking to any media. They pointed out that it would not be in their best interest since by allowing access by one media outlet they would have to allow others.

Shreveport, Louisiana

The Illinois Gas Dealers Association has continually misled us on threatened strike and shutdown actions during this gas crunch.

Chicago, Illinois

During the height of the gasoline shortage in California, we had difficulty obtaining concrete explanations from business and government. No one could or would provide one single cause. Business [oil companies] seemed most reluctant to talk with reporters. That may be somewhat understandable in that many politicians did not hesitate to blame the oil companies for virtually all energy and economic problems. I suspect some business officials had the impression the media had already "loaded the deck" against them.

Los Angeles, California

We in Tulsa are so close to the energy companies that we find ourselves surrounded by industry advocates. When we need local reaction to routine energy stories, we have literally dozens of qualified authorities sympathetic to the industry available to talk to, but very few qualified authorities who disagree. Most area politicians and government officials are generally pro-industry. As a result, day-to-day coverage of energy in Tulsa tends to reflect that situation.

Tulsa, Oklahoma

The oil companies still are ill-equipped, to put it kindly, to react to the energy story. Despite the fact that this is the oil capital of the world, there appears to be a reluctance on the part of the oil executives who have the answers to appear on television, especially in spot situations, to react to international or national developments in energy matters. In addition, the media contacts in oil companies frequently exhibit a startling lack of appreciation for our problems. Most are either print conscious or incompetent.

Houston, Texas

On the issue of energy, we have faced the problem that most news organizations must have faced in recent months. It is difficult to know who and what to believe. It is difficult to get reliable and impartial statistical information. Almost everything we have reported and been told has been proven wrong by events. It is no wonder that the public has so little belief in an "energy crisis." They have been consistently misled and misinformed by officials on all sides of the issue. There isn't anyone out there telling the truth. Perhaps it's because no one knows the truth.

Boston, Massachusetts

Once again, as at Three Mile Island, broadcast journalists had run up against the deliberate secrecy and misrepresentations of industry and the apparent inability of government to explain and regulate. And radio and TV were unable to penetrate the situation on their own.

What should have been the simplest question was perhaps the most elusive: Was there enough oil? Oil company executives, the only ones who knew, claimed in interview after interview that there was not. Clifton Garvin, chairman of Exxon, told CBS's George Herman on *Face the Nation:*

> Mr. Herman, we do have a shortage in this country. Defining "shortage" to mean we don't have quite as much as apparently what those of us in the public want to use. Our basic problem is that we've reached the point where the producing countries outside of the U.S. and Canada are not quite willing to produce as much oil as we need in the short term, and therefore as long as they keep that oil tight, we are going to be facing a shortage.

The immediate cause of the gas lines in May, according to Garvin and several other oil company chiefs, was the revolution in Iran. The chaos resulting from the fall of the Shah and the rise of the Ayatollah Khomeini in February had reduced Iranian production of crude oil from 6 million barrels a day to 1 million. Even with increased Saudi Arabian production, U.S. imports would still be short by 600,000 barrels a day, or 3.3 percent of our needs.

John O'Leary, deputy secretary of energy, confirmed this view of the crisis on the *CBS Morning News* the second week in May, as the gas lines in California grew:

> We're finally beginning to get the effects of the Iranian outage. It takes a long time for the ships to stop coming to our shores, and they finally have stopped coming in sufficient numbers to cause our

crude supplies to be critically low. And we're finally finding that the refiners are not able to make enough gasoline to go around. And in the meantime, all during the period when every day we were treated with headlines of the Iranian crisis, the gasoline consumption of this country has been rising and rising and rising. In January and February, for example, it was about seven percent above where it was a year ago.

But contrary to O'Leary's claims, figures from the Organization of Economic Cooperation and Development in Paris showed that U.S. oil consumption from January to April 1979 was nearly 1 percent *below* consumption in the same period in 1978. It was up to the broadcasters who had seen oil "crises" come and go to reconcile such contradictions and to put them in perspective. They reminded viewers that an oil glut had followed the 1973–74 crisis. Similarly, in April 1977, soon after Congress eased price controls on natural gas, a seeming scarcity had turned overnight into abundance.

At the end of July 1979, when several OPEC members—Algeria, Nigeria, and Kuwait—announced cutbacks in their crude oil production because of decreased demand and Saudi Arabia's increased production, the broadcasters once again were the ones who raised the possibility of a glut following the shortage.

The oil companies and the Energy Department had a ready explanation for the stories about the gluts. Said Exxon's Garvin:

Last year and the year before, there was a surplus in production capability around the world of about 10 percent, and those in the media came to refer to this as a glut. It's not a glut. It was brought about primarily because of recession in Europe and things of this nature that knocked down the demand for oil.

Hanfling of the Energy Department added:

> To understand the true significance of Iran, one must go back to the tranquil days of last September [1978]—less than a year ago—during which time the Department of Energy principally attempted to rebut the spate of stories and statements hailing "gluts" of oil and natural gas. The drumbeats from the media were of the glut of oil on the West Coast, the sudden glut of natural gas, and the emergence of Mexico as an oil superpower. A prominent economist was making headlines with the thesis that there was 12 million barrels per day of excess oil production capacity in the world. During that perverse season, man was biting dog with regard to the energy crisis every day. The crisis had gone away, said the headlines, and surpluses were the order of the day.
>
> Just a few months later, we find that one hitch in our world oil supply system, the temporary disappearance of Iran as a supplier, brings us to the brink of crisis.
>
> Where are the gluts of "yestermonth"? The glut peddlers now purvey gloom and doom. Where they once erred on the side of sanguinity, they now miss the entire point of the Iranian shortfall.

If one could believe the oil companies and the Energy Department, oil gluts were a mere fabrication of the media. The implication was that broadcasters' fantasies prevented the American people from accepting the reality of the 1979 gas crisis. But the broadcasters had good reason to be skeptical. They had dug up and reported to viewers a number of crucial facts and figures that simply did not jibe with oil company and Energy Department versions of the 1979 "crisis."

While the oil companies were blaming the shortage on Iran and the inaccessibility of crude oil, they were importing 4.6 percent more oil in the first half of 1979 than they did in the first half of 1978. World oil production rose 4.4 percent in that period. An FTC staff memo dated May 30 noted that "gasoline supplies in 1979 were up by 4–8 percent, depending on the time period, over 1978. Net supply of gasoline in April was particularly plentiful compared to the previous April (up by 22.9 percent)."* And yet, despite the increase in crude oil supplies, the oil companies had cut back deliveries of gasoline to U.S. service stations by 10 to 15 percent, according to a General Accounting Office study. Even the American Petroleum Institute, the industry association, admitted that the oil companies had delivered 9.8 percent less gas to the market place in May 1979 than they had a year earlier.

Though the shortage at the pumps had not yet eased, in the first week in June broadcasters reported that the nation's refineries were operating at only 84 percent of

---

*In January 1980, a report prepared by the House Government Operations Subcommittee on Commerce revealed that the Department of Energy had "deliberately withheld significant information about a substantial February increase in oil imports from the Congress and the public because," as one Department official put it, " 'it would have been embarrassing.' " The report also stated that Treasury Secretary Michael Blumenthal had been advised by his aides in late January 1979 to keep secret a Treasury Department study that concluded that the cutback in Iranian oil production did not lead to a crude oil shortage in the United States.

their capacity—a situation that Energy Secretary James Schlesinger called "disappointing, troublesome, and irritating."

The Energy Department disclosed that it would review seven of the eighteen largest oil companies—including Texaco and Mobil—to find out whether the decline in output at the refineries was legitimate or not. The oil companies denied that they were withholding crude oil—in tankers, storage tanks, refineries, or anywhere else. But only three weeks after Schlesinger's uncharacteristic outburst, production at the nation's refineries jumped to nearly 90 percent of capacity.

So it went in the spring and summer of 1979. Broadcast journalists had to rely largely on data supplied by the oil companies. Without subpoena power, there was no way to penetrate the oil companies. Nor was there any way to verify the figures independently. Even the government, which was charged with the responsibility of regulating the oil giants, was not able or willing to audit the industry's reports on a broad scale or to overcome its sophisticated legal stonewalling.*

Since it was impossible for broadcasters to find out precisely how much oil the big companies had in their tanks, they spent much of their time reporting on the subject that concerned viewers most directly—price. In seven months from December 1978 to July 1979, the

*The government seemed reluctant to take on the responsibility of providing independent figures on the oil industry. In December 1978, Representative John Dingell, chairman of the House Energy and Power Subcommittee, told NBC's *Meet the Press*, "One of the problems we have is that this administration and the prior administration have sternly refused to go out and gather the data as required by . . . statute." The Energy Department first published independent weekly statistics on the oil industry in January 1980.

average price for a gallon of regular gas jumped from
67.5 cents to 91.1 cents, for a gallon of home heating oil
from 52.6 cents to 73.9 cents.

Seventy-seven percent of the American people, according to one Gallup poll, thought the oil companies
had cooked up the shortage simply to drive up prices.
In May, gas suddenly had been scarce, and by the end
of July it was just as suddenly plentiful again. But no-
body had been able to uncover a smoking gun—a tape,
a document: real proof that the oil companies had deliberately created a crisis. So the broadcasters gave a
selection of views. They straightforwardly reported the
opinion of the oil companies and many Americans that
OPEC was to blame—it had, after all, jacked up its prices
42 percent by the end of the first six months of 1979.
And they also presented without much fuss the contention of people like Barry Bosworth, director of the
Council on Wage and Price Stability, that price-goug-
ing local dealers had taken advantage of the situation to
rip off consumers.

But when the networks reported the quarterly
profits of oil companies and interviewed energy acti-
vists who suggested a link between high profits and
high prices, they found themselves embroiled in controversy. The broadcasters had not done any muckrak-
ing to get the profit figures. They had merely quoted
statistics that were made public every three months. In
the first quarter, the networks told the American people, the earnings of the twenty-three leading oil companies jumped by 58 percent over 1978. In the second
quarter, they vaulted another 69 percent to $5.3 bil-
lion. And third-quarter advances were even greater.
Texaco led the industry with a 211 percent gain over
the third quarter in 1978, followed by Sohio (191 per-

cent), Mobil (131 percent), Exxon (118 percent), Gulf (97 percent), Phillips (65 percent), Standard Oil of Indiana (49 percent), and Arco (45 percent).

Instantly the oil companies responded that these breathtaking profits were not excessive,* and an old antagonist, feisty Mobil, took the offensive against the television networks. A week and a half after Mobil, the world's second largest oil company, had reported its third-quarter profits, it shelled out about $325,000 to buy two-page ads in the *New York Times* and eleven other newspapers, and a single page in four magazines. Under the heading "19 dull and unsensational facts about our profits the TV networks didn't tell you—and won't allow us to tell you," the ads charged that the TV news reports on Mobil's profits had deceived the public with "simplistic sensationalism." Crucial information had been omitted, Mobil argued, leaving viewers without "an intelligent perspective." The ads singled out a CBS story by Ray Brady as "the worst, the most unfair, report on Mobil earnings that we've ever seen," calling it "an irresponsible flight of fantasy."

The story, which was pegged to the announcement of Mobil's and several other oil companies' third-quarter profits, said in part, "Mobil, like other international oil companies, says the big profits were not made here, but in foreign markets, which would mean that foreign

---

*But past oil company profits were already being challenged as excessive in court. The Energy Department charged that fifteen major refiners had overcharged the public by $6.4 billion from 1973 through 1976. Later it brought formal charges against nine more major refiners, accusing them of overcharging another $1.18 billion in the same time period. The administration said the investigation would continue and could eventually result in allegations that consumers paid up to $25 billion too much for petroleum products from 1973 to 1979.

consumers were the ones getting hit." It went on to quote oil company critics who described a clever book-keeping technique by which oil companies could shuffle some of their domestic earnings into the foreign column.

CBS stood by its report, saying that it "dealt not pri-marily with Mobil, but with the international oil com-panies' method of reporting their profits. . . . It labeled the opinion of oil company critics as precisely that and not as the opinion of CBS News." The network claimed that it had unsuccessfully tried to get an on-camera interview with a Mobil spokesman on the day the story aired, and it concluded, "CBS News will continue to report on all sectors of the energy industry, including Mobil, and will continue to reflect the news of a wide variety of observers on the question of oil company profits."

Although not specifically named in the Mobil ads, ABC stood by its report on third-quarter profits. NBC made no official comment, but a few days after the Mobil ad appeared, the network's energy correspon-dent, Andrea Mitchell, noted in a panel discussion on energy coverage that Mobil was not always so forth-coming with information as it purported to be. Just that week the Energy Department had accused Mobil of overcharging the public by $274.7 million from 1973 to 1976, and Mobil had made only one official available to reporters to read a fifteen-second speech. "I believe they have no defense for that kind of behavior," said Mitchell, "especially in the same week they took on CBS News."

Mobil did make one point that broadcasters were hard put to refute: TV newscasts simply did not have time to report complex energy stories in detail or to put them in proper perspective. The networks maintained silence on this issue, but a *Broadcasting* editorial expressed the only defense they could muster:

> There were more words in the Mobil double truck than can be recited in the whole of a CBS Evening News half hour of the kind that contained but a short piece on oil company earnings. The disparity in length between television news and print journalism is a condition that responsible broadcast journalists regret but accept as inherent in the business.

The networks could alleviate this unfortunate time squeeze, Mobil asserted, by allowing it to express its views on the issues in paid ads:

> When TV news omits or distorts important facts, neither we nor anyone else is able to set the record straight, as we often can in the press with letters to the editor or signed articles.
>
> The TV networks, moreover, have refused to sell us air time to present our point of view, even when we offered to buy additional time so that those who differed with us could reply at our expense.
>
> The casualty in all this has been the public's understanding of important issues. Television's information blackout is, we suggest, the real "rip-off" of the American people.

The question of whether or not so-called issue ads should be permitted on TV had been debated since 1974, when the networks had rejected a Mobil ad about drilling for oil beneath beaches. More recently, in 1978, Mobil had sought to refute what it called "gross misrepresentations" made in an August 8 *20/20* segment on natural gas deregulation. It had asked ABC to air its filmed reply either on *20/20* or as a commercial. The network had refused, saying only, "ABC does not sell time for comment on controversial issues."

The subject came up again in 1979, when Kaiser Aluminum and Chemical Corporation tried to buy network time for three seemingly innocuous commercials, including one about the energy crisis, and was turned down. "Our judgment was that if we ran these we would be open to the Fairness Doctrine," said NBC. ABC explained once more, "We do not sell time for the discussion of controversial issues that are of public importance. We feel those issues are best left for treatment by our public affairs and news departments." And CBS added, "It's been a policy that we do not accept editorial advertising," which would allow "those with the most money to speak the loudest."

Despite the protests of Mobil, the networks stuck to their no-issue-ads stance.* The only energy ads that got on the air seemed to be about automobiles with high miles-per-gallon claims, fuel-efficient motor oil, and companies and utilities pushing conservation.

What emerged from all these inconclusive encounters between media, industry, and government was the realization that the United States desperately needed a comprehensive and workable energy policy. Why it didn't have one was fundamentally a political story. Broadcasters who had concentrated their reporting on the mechanics of the gas crisis and the culpability (or

---

*In December, Ted Turner offered to sell commercial time on his superstation, WTBS, to corporations, political candidates, and others denied access by the networks. His price for a half-hour message in prime time reaching 3.5 million homes was $7,500, compared to as much as $150,000 on the networks.

innocence) of the oil companies now shifted their focus to the politics of energy.

Jimmy Carter in midsummer began to dominate the newscasts with his ineffectual attempts to mobilize the nation, his problems in pushing an energy program through Congress, his dwindling chances for reelection in 1980. There was the canceled July 5 "major television speech" and the ten-day retreat to Camp David, when a parade of important leaders from all walks of life were summoned to see the President, though to the TV cameras he remained invisible. There was the coming down from the Maryland mountains, with yet another energy program drafted by a task force of eighty to one hundred people from various government departments. And there was the major July 15 speech that preempted, among other things, an episode of *Moses the Lawgiver* on CBS and attracted a TV audience of 65 million, the largest for a Carter speech since November 1977, when he had also spoken on the energy crisis. This night he preached on the "crisis of confidence" and outlined his new energy program, a potpourri of ideas that had been adrift in Congress for some time— the windfall profits tax, limits on oil imports, standby authority to ration gas, a call for the public to do its bit, more money for mass transit, and more money to help the poor with fuel bills. There were a few fresh ideas, too: an independent Energy Security Corporation to stimulate production of synthetic fuels and an Energy Mobilization Board to cut red tape for key energy projects. (The total price tag: a staggering $142 billion over a decade, more than was spent during the entire American involvement in Vietnam.)

Hard on the President's cry to the colors came the

Carter version of the Saturday Night Massacre—five cabinet members ousted* and Hamilton Jordan elevated to the old H. R. Haldeman chief-of-staff position —and the announcement that high-level employees would be evaluated in glorified report cards. The President's appeal to join hands to lick the energy crisis, reporters surmised, was merely part of a deliberate image face-lift for an unpopular first-term president looking ahead to the 1980 elections.

For the broadcast journalist, what had begun as a simple visual story on the gas lines had grown into the complicated and elusive story of world oil supplies and finally merged into the shadowboxing of presidential politics.

Some in the administration wanted the broadcasters to help rally the country around the President and forge a national consensus on energy. Robert Hanfling of the Energy Department told the AP broadcasters:

> The solution of our energy problem, on a crash basis or otherwise, is a matter of national will. . . . As of yet, however, we have not even developed a national consensus that there is a problem, much less what to do about it.
>
> The press, of course, does and will play a pivotal role in the development of that consensus or the failure to develop it. . . .
>
> We recognize that in the wake of Vietnam and Watergate, there is a new cynicism in the land directed at the credibility of any established insti-

*They were Joseph Califano of Health, Education, and Welfare; James Schlesinger of Energy; Brock Adams of Transportation; Michael Blumenthal of Treasury; and Griffin Bell of Justice. Only Bell had been planning to resign at the time.

tution, especially government. In the energy field, already more complex than the average reporter feels comfortable about, ample temptations exist to oversimplify, to take sides, to seek scapegoats, to ignore the motivations of the critics. We are living in a time when if a scientist reveals evidence that the sun still rises in the east, a reporter will look until he finds another scientist who swears it rises in the west. . . .

If energy has placed a large burden on government to produce fair, effective policies founded on facts, the burden falling on the press to report those developments accurately is even larger.

To some journalists, Hanfling's message had uncomfortable implications: report accurately, but don't destroy the national will by giving too much time to critics who disagree with the President's approach. Broadcasters did not embrace this cheerleader role. Instead, they viewed the President's energy program as a political issue and dutifully reported the rising clamor of voices attacking it: oil companies jumping on the windfall profits tax; environmentalists blasting the Energy Mobilization Board as a means to bypass clean air and water laws; health officials complaining that synthetic fuel production would leave a trail of carcinogenic wastes on the land and dangerous amounts of carbon dioxide in the air; economists questioning the wisdom of such massive spending in an inflationary time; presidential aspirants Baker, Anderson, Connally, and Brown getting in their licks; ecologist-author Barry Commoner announcing the formation of the Citizens Party to put forward in the 1980 elections a different energy platform based on nationalization of the oil companies.

Carter made a couple of attempts to recruit the help of the networks in promoting his energy program. On September 13, he and media adviser Gerald Rafshoon met for an hour in the White House with the chairmen and presidents of CBS, NBC, and ABC. Carter asked the executives for suggestions about how to get across the need for an energy program. They reportedly discussed the possibility of energy-related TV specials and the use of energy themes on entertainment shows. Presidential assistant Jack Watson had proposed earlier in a memo that the White House try to persuade Walter Cronkite to host a special explaining ways to conserve energy—an idea that never panned out.

But Carter never seriously expected to change the broadcasters' attitude toward him. Having decided at Camp David that it was time to bypass the reporters who covered him regularly and to establish direct dialogue with the American people, the President embarked on a series of weekly regional news conferences, back-porch conversations with citizens, and town meetings to drum up support for his energy plan and for his own reelection. Simultaneously, he cut down on regular White House briefings and on formal Washington news conferences that he had held twice a month since taking office.

But the President's dream of national unity and consensus on energy was not to be. Congress was hopelessly divided (by the time the August recess rolled around, not a single element of the President's plan had been passed*), the public was confused, and the Presi-

---

*By the end of 1979, Congress had passed watered-down versions of a couple of elements of Carter's plan—standby authority to ration gas and financial aid to the poor to help with higher fuel bills—and had reached a tentative compromise on a windfall profits tax.

dent was frustrated and worried about Senator Edward Kennedy's challenge to his renomination.

Ironically, it was Senator George McGovern—the principal figure in one of the most disastrous campaigns in the history of American presidential politics—who realized the power of television as a unifying medium and offered one of the more interesting suggestions to break the impasse:

> Before we impose rationing or channel billions of dollars in new tax money into the oil companies on behalf of President Carter's latest proposal, we need to find out exactly how the oil industry operates. It is imperative that the government initiate a full-scale investigation, coupled with public hearings, into the operations of the nation's oil companies.
>
> This is the prerequisite to an effective energy policy.
>
> And without it, the restoration of public confidence President Carter hopes for will never occur. . . .
>
> The Watergate committee hearings were critical to the country's ability to reach a consensus on the political transition we faced in 1973.
>
> Until we turn the same light onto the oil industry, we will not know what is needed to meet the new conditions of world oil supply, and we will not obtain public confidence in what we ask people to do in the name of a new energy future. . . .
>
> This must be a serious, well-staffed, and televised investigation. . . . The unique potential of television to lay bare the realities of an issue can lead us to a democratic solution that can no longer be deferred.

While the McGovern proposal was a tribute to television's potential power, it was no compliment to newscasters. It was a frank admission that everyone from TV commentators to national leaders to the guy at the gas pump was confused about oil. Surely some of the confusion resulted from oil company obfuscation and manipulation. Some of it stemmed from the President's mistakes and his inability to communicate. Some came from the Energy Department's lack of direction and from Congress's wishy-washy buckling to special interests. And a large part of the problem was the American people's own reluctance to face the depressing facts and change a life-style that a world with shrinking natural resources and a growing population could no longer sustain.

But McGovern's proposal also implied that news media—and particularly broadcasters from whom most of the people got their news—had not done their job as well as they might have. They had failed to analyze and clarify the issues in a way that the American people could understand. They had allowed presidential politics and image-making to divert them and obscure some of the basic choices to be made. The nightly news had flickered by on TV screens all over the land and added up to a blur. The broadcasters had tried in specials to give sorely needed perspective to what was happening, but they had fallen short of the mark.

Now a prominent senator was asking that TV newscasters be bypassed altogether, so that the medium itself could be used only as a vehicle for a special government investigation. If it could be done, it was possible that the people would eventually understand and begin to believe again. Predictably, McGovern's proposal was met with as much enthusiasm as an empty gas tank.

10/Gadgets and Gimmicks: The Communications Revolution

> There is a revolution going on in communications—
> a technological revolution that is changing both the
> game and the names.
>
> *Broadcasting* magazine, January 1, 1979
>
> The kind of storm that swept Dorothy off to Oz is
> about to hit the old broadcasting industry.
>
> *The New York Times Magazine*, August 19, 1979

It may have taken a decade longer than expected, but as the 1970s ended, the oft-heralded "communications revolution" finally seemed to have arrived. According to House Communications Subcommittee Chairman Lionel Van Deerlin, the 1980s would usher in changes that "will transform not only the face of broadcasting, but the lives of Americans as profoundly as the Industrial Revolution of the nineteenth century."

Such extravagant pronouncements had been made regularly over the past ten years, and most Americans had continued to watch the same networks, the same local stations, the same kinds of programming, and the same commercials, with only slight variations. By 1979, however, many of the "new technologies" that had been experiments or dreams at the beginning of the decade—cable, pay TV, subscription TV, satellites, superstations, fiber optics, video tape recorders, video disks, two-way TV, teletext, earth stations, and other even more outlandish developments—were workable realities. Much of the hardware had been perfected, the market price had begun to drop, and consumers were buying the services in growing numbers. How this ferment in the communications world would affect broadcasters and their news operations depended on the actions of the FCC, on consumer acceptance of the new equipment, and ultimately on the quality and diversity of programming the new technologies brought into viewers' homes.

The spectacular mushrooming of cable was the most convincing bit of evidence that a new era in communications was indeed at hand. Since 1968, cable had grown from a means of improving reception of conventional TV in less than 5 percent of TV homes to an independent technology offering a wide variety of services to 43 million American TV viewers, 20 percent of the total. The number of cable systems had doubled nationwide from 2,000 to 4,100, with subscribers leaping from 2.8 million to an estimated 15 million at the end of 1979. And the number of subscribers to pay cable, the medium's box office programming, had leaped to over 5 million.

Overall, the cable industry was expanding at a rate of 10 percent a year, and a survey of viewer attitudes done for the National Cable Television Association suggested an abundant future. Forty-four percent of those interviewed expressed "high interest" in receiving cable service, and significantly, the youngest viewers in the sample, aged eighteen to twenty-four, were the most interested (62 percent).

As of 1978, the total ad revenues of cable amounted to only $8.5 million, compared to $8.1 billion reaped by television broadcasters the same year. But whenever cable reached 30 percent of the nation's TV households, the industry could be considered competitive with other media for advertising. In 1970, industry pundits had predicted such penetration would be unthinkable before 1995, but a decade later they considered it attainable as early as 1981.

Even without massive advertising, cable had become a big business on its own, bringing in $1.4 billion in revenues in 1978. The competition for cable franchises, slack for years in most urban centers, had turned "cutthroat, no-holds-barred," according to Harold Horn, executive director of the Cable TV Information Center. "There's hardly a major city that isn't in the midst of this," he said. Twenty-nine different companies were vying for the right to cable up four of New York City's boroughs, and nine had submitted bids for Philadelphia franchises. Increasingly, several cable systems were having to share the major markets. In Houston, for example, five companies were granted franchises in 1979, and as many as twenty cable systems were operating simultaneously in eight counties throughout the nation.

General Electric, Times-Mirror, Warner Communications, Cox, Storer, and Getty Oil were a few of the large corporations joining pioneers Time, Inc., and Teleprompter in sinking big chunks of capital into cable industries. A report released by Warburg Paribas Becker, Inc., a New York–based investment banking firm, predicted that more than $500 million would be loaned to cable companies in 1979 by banks and insurance companies. A single applicant for the New York franchises, Warner Communications, anticipated an investment of $400 million should it be successful in winning the franchises. And if any further proof of cable's attractiveness as an investment was needed, it came in May 1979 when 125 representatives of seventy-eight lending organizations descended upon the National Cable Television Association convention, combing the crowd of 6,300 for potential borrowers.

"Cable is at last taking off," proclaimed a May 1979 cover story in *Time* magazine, hardly a disinterested party. And the trend in Washington toward deregulation looked as if it would help the industry fly even higher. The long-term lobbying efforts of broadcasters were being ignored as government restrictions that had in the past severely limited cable's program diversity were lifted one by one. In April, the Supreme Court overthrew the FCC requirement that cable systems provide public access channels. In May, the FCC itself began to shed its role as protector of over-the-air broadcasters by getting rid of a rule that barred cable operators from using the same programming as local broadcasters. And perhaps more important, it proposed a new rule allowing cable operators to pick up signals from as many distant broadcast stations as they wished. FCC Commissioner Joseph Fogarty voiced the new view from Washington:

> In the past, the FCC has tried to "integrate" emerging new technologies, in particular cable TV, into the over-the-air broadcasting status quo. The commission has done so ostensibly in the interest of preserving the "localism" of its broadcast allocation and assignment policies and according to some notion of the "public interest." . . .
> I think this policy and regulatory approach has

been a gross mistake. Something more than mere conjecture or intuitive assumptions should be required before we impose regulatory constraints and burdens on one industry or technology in favor of another. I think the most important thing for the commission to do in an era of explosive innovation is to get out of the way, to adopt a wait-and-see attitude and posture, rather than to rush to regulatory judgments. We should rely on the marketplace and competitive forces to serve the public interest in program diversity until experience, not speculation, shows that this approach is inadequate.

This hands-off attitude, which ultimately fell short of realization, was the overall theme of Lionel Van Deerlin's proposed rewrite of the Communications Act, a hymn to deregulation of broadcasting and cable alike. Among other things, it would require cable operators to negotiate for program rights in a free competitive market. Previously, under a formula established by Congress, cable operators had been paying owners of programs minimal copyright fees—$12 million total in 1978, or about 10 percent of their revenues, as opposed to broadcasters who paid $2 billion or 40 to 45 percent of their revenues for program material. The Van Deerlin bill also proposed that local communities be free to bargain with cable operators to arrive at a fair franchising agreement. Federal deregulation, it seemed, would only put cable operators at the mercy of innumerable state and local legislators. Most threatening of all to cable operators, the bill would allow telephone companies, including the world's largest corporation, AT&T, to enter the cable field, where heretofore they had been forbidden.

Cable operators complained that these provisions of the Van Deerlin bill would kill their blossoming industry. But Van Deerlin had little sympathy. He told the NCTA annual convention that he had heard the same tune from broadcasters, common carriers, and others affected by the proposed legislation: "All I want is a fair advantage." The House Communications Subcommittee chairman said, "The cable industry has come of age. Like your competitors, the broadcasters, you too have discovered how to use the regulatory fences to your advantage." He made it clear that he no longer saw cable as "a diminutive David, struggling against an army of Goliaths that include broadcasters, telephone companies, program owners, and state and local governments."

For their part, broadcasters fought both the FCC and Van Deerlin's attempts to deregulate cable. The National Association of Broadcasters urged the FCC to adopt a rule that would require cable operators to obtain consent from the owner of the original broadcaster of a program before it could be retransmitted. While that effort failed, lobbying by broadcasters and others finally forced Van Deerlin in July to withdraw his rewritten Communications Act.

The NAB worried that cable would lure viewers away from over-the-air stations, thus decreasing their advertising revenues. It produced a study by Charles River Associates that concluded, "There is almost a direct correlation between audience loss to cable and drops in station revenues. If a station loses 10 percent of its audience, it can expect to lose from 8 percent to 11 percent of its revenues. . . . The evidence is now on the record. It is conclusive."

But a voluminous two-year study by the FCC's Cable

Television Bureau predicted that cable would not be a "significant" threat to broadcasters. Cable TV Bureau Chief Philip Verveer said that his task force found no evidence to corroborate the NAB's contention that cable had already harmed several stations in small markets. In the short term, according to the study, stations would lose less than 1 percent of their audience and revenues as a result of deregulation of cable. Over the long term, it predicted that cable would reach a maximum penetration of 48 percent of TV households and that some local stations could lose up to 9 percent of their audience and revenues. On the other hand, in certain markets where reception of over-the-air signals was poor, cable had helped broadcasters reach new and larger audiences. The study concluded, "While some TV stations will undeniably face the prospect of increased competition as a result of cable, few, if any, TV stations are likely to experience a reduction in real income."

Even if cable was not yet a serious competitor to broadcasters, a few isolated examples proved that it definitely had the potential to be. A. C. Nielsen's first major study of 5,000 pay cable subscribers, conducted in February 1979, revealed that they frequently preferred new movies on the pay channels to competing prime-time fare on the regular broadcasting networks. For instance, on February 25, Home Box Office's *Looking for Mr. Goodbar* was seen in more pay cable subscribers' homes than ABC's *Roots II,* NBC's *Sound of Music,* and CBS's *Challenge of the Sexes.* Over the whole month, 16 percent of the viewers surveyed tuned in to pay channels during prime time, while 19 percent chose NBC, 20 percent went for CBS, and 31 percent watched ABC.

In another test of cable's potential drawing power, Warner Cable's experimental Qube system in Columbus, Ohio, reported that on the average at any given time in 1978, half its subscribers were tuned to the standard network channels, 25 percent to imported distant signals, and 25 percent to Qube's own origination channels. An over-the-air TV news director from Fort Myers, Florida, a three-station market, told the Du-Pont-Columbia Survey that during the May sweeps rating period, local cable channels as a group (referred to by the rating services as "other") had attracted audiences that matched those of each of the local over-the-air stations. "At times [they] even [did] better," he wrote. 'Other' has become a serious competitor."

On occasion, cable contended with the networks for original programming. For instance, ABC won the bidding for the 1984 Los Angeles summer Olympic games with an offer of $225 million, but its stiffest competition, reported *Ad Age,* came from a cable outfit. A $190 million bid by Norman Lear and Jerry Perenchio's T.A.T. Communications topped both CBS and NBC.

The networks constantly reminded themselves and others of what they perceived as a programming advantage over their poorer cable brethren. Gene Jankowski, president of CBS/Broadcast Group, told his affiliates in May:

> At a time when some self-styled soothsayers are predicting that new technologies will bring an end to the free system of communications that has served this country so well for so long, I think it very important to state that people don't buy technology. The public is far more concerned with what appears on the screen than how it gets there. . . .

Beyond sports, what do these extra signals provide? For the most part, old movies and off-network reruns and even some dusted off, old PBS material. If we announced a comparable schedule, someone would be calling for a congressional investigation, and the critics would be looking upon television as the light that failed.

I truly wish that there was an infinite quantity of good programming available, but there isn't. Adding signals to the market place will not be adding to choice. Diversity already exists, in terms of offering the viewer a choice of programs. But "more" is not always "better" and in no way does "quantity" always mean "quality." And with all the marvels of new technology, no one has figured out how to view more than one program at a time.

That there were no remaining program opportunities ignored by the networks, as Jankowski implied, was open to challenge, particularly in the field of news and public affairs. But as far as news programming was concerned, it was equally true that cable so far provided, in FCC Chairman Charles Ferris's words, not a choice but an echo, and a very faint one at that. In a survey conducted by NCTA, only 20 percent of the responding cable systems that originated programs said that they produced local news shows. Many more (about 86 percent) carried twenty-four-hour-a-day news summaries prepared by AP, UPI, and Reuters.

One plan for an all-day video news service, Home Box Office's NewsPlus, fizzled for lack of advertisers and cable homes on the line. And Viacom International's magazine-style *What's Up, America?*—which was supposed to help fill the documentary gap on cable —ended up leaning more toward entertainment than news. The hour-long pilot show, aired in October 1978, featured segments on honeymoon hotels in the Poconos, an erotic bakery in New York, and an improvisation group in Los Angeles, and was followed by two others that included takeouts on such topics as the Miss Nude California Pageant, a twins convention, female boxers, and BB gun warriors.

Cable systems were no longer required to offer public access programming, but many still did. Although only a small part of cable's overall schedule, public access was the source of some of its strongest news and public affairs programming. In contrast to local broadcasters, public access channels could devote the time necessary for gavel-to-gavel coverage of community meetings, for politicians to answer constituents' questions, for specialized ethnic news, and for thorough explorations of important local issues. Manhattan Cable, for instance, designated four channels for public access and provided a combined total of forty hours of programming on them per day, including coverage of community board meetings, phone-in office hours for council members, and Chinese language news. Manhattan Cable polled its 105,000 subscribers and found that an impressive one third of them watched the access channels regularly.

Like several other operators, Viacom's Marin 11 in San Rafael, California, gave viewers an opportunity to participate in the political process. A program on Marin County's transit problems, for instance, featured a taped documentary, a live discussion with officials, and phone calls from viewers. Berks Community Television in Reading, Pennsylvania, also offered live interactive programming. It effectively used two-way video and audio, giving people from several neighborhoods around the city a chance to interact face-to-face on a split screen or to call in on the phone.

The most ambitious, expensive, and widely publicized attempt to involve the public in two-way television was Warner Cable Corporation's system in Columbus, Ohio. While the two-year-old Columbus Qube operation produced no local hard news programs, it did offer to its 30,000 subscribers a popular weekday morning show called *Columbus Alive,* loosely patterned after NBC's *Today.* Its unique contribution, however, was that it allowed viewers to register their views on public affairs programs instantaneously. The system worked with PBS to produce two *Advocates* programs, in which controversial issues were debated. The home audiences gave instant feedback to the participants by "touching in" on little black boxes wired to a central computer. A town meeting in suburban Upper Arlington was attended by 125 people in person and another 2,200 over Qube. The home viewers responded to questions from the city planning commission and could request recognition to speak by punching buttons. A remarkable 96 percent of those watching the town meeting at the end of two and a half hours voted that they would like to participate in such a setup again.

Qube's unique capabilities were exploited in other news and public affairs programs, the most notable of which was an instant poll conducted on July 15, 1979, immediately following Jimmy Carter's energy speech (described in chapter 9).* On other occasions, FDA

---

*Albert H. Cantril, president of the National Council on Public Polls, criticized NBC's airing of Qube's instant poll. He claimed that Qube viewers were not even representative of Columbus, let alone the United States.

Commissioner Donald Kennedy asked 3,000 viewers for advice on food labeling over Qube and declared the experience a refreshing change from normal public hearings, which were packed with lobbyists. Ralph Nader polled Qube subscribers on consumer issues and particularly on their views about television, so that he could carry the results to the Van Deerlin Committee considering the Communications Act rewrite at the time; 39 percent complained that commercial television most lacked cultural and educational programming, and 46 percent said that they did not have an adequate opportunity to express their views on TV. Tip O'Neill also appeared several times on Qube to get instant feedback on various issues facing Congress. And Gloria Steinem asked for viewers' opinions on the Equal Rights Amendment.

Warner Vice-President for Public Affairs Leo Murray called Qube "an instrument of democracy" and foresaw a day when citizens would vote in elections over two-way TV: "Can you imagine the possibilities? All the people who can't get out to the polls, and all the people who won't go out to them?"

Qube's computer had obvious advantages, but FCC Chairman Charles Ferris, addressing the Audit Bureau of Circulation meeting in November 1979, voiced doubts about instant polls and their chilling effect on the political process: "History is full of examples of unpopular decisions that were ultimately proven correct. But what judgment could withstand the pressure of the instantaneously expressed electronic opinion of many millions?"

Although by the end of 1979 Warner was still losing money on its initial $20 million investment in Qube in Columbus, it started to build similar systems in Houston and suburban Cincinnati. It had applied for additional franchises in Pittsburgh, New York, and other cities, and it planned to refit its one-way system in Akron, Ohio. To help finance this massive undertaking, Warner tried to sell a half interest in all its operations to American Express for $175 million. The FCC scotched the deal in December 1979 because of cross-ownership violations by two directors of American Express who were also directors of General Electric and the New York Times Company, owners of television stations in ten communities served by Warner cable systems. The two directors then resigned and the deal went through on December 31. The company was renamed Warner Amex Cable Communications.

Whether Qube's two-way potential would expand the definition of news and public affairs programming remained to be seen. An equally significant development was the increased use of satellites to distribute programming to cable systems and over-the-air stations. In 1979, about 2,000 cable operators owned "earth stations" to receive signals from satellites. A number of small satellite "networks" had sprung up to help fulfill cable's long-awaited and as yet unrealized promise as an alternative source of diverse specialized programs. Qube offered an all-day children's network called Nickelodeon. Cinemerica Satellite Network unveiled a service directed at viewers over fifty years old. The fledgling Black Entertainment Television network was planning to bounce two hours a week of black-oriented programming off the "bird" to cable operators who signed up for the service. The Spanish International Network, SIN, was providing one hundred hours of programming a week to stations and cable operators serving 2 million Hispanic-speaking households in the

United States. And UPI-Newstime, a twenty-four-hour audiovisual news service consisting of still photos and audio "actualities," was being transmitted over Satcom I to 103 cable systems nationwide.

Using an interesting mix of satellite technology, cable, and toll-free phone banks, the nonprofit Center for Non-Broadcast Television and the International Association of Machinists and Aerospace Workers presented a provocative ninety-minute program in April called "The Lost Million: Is American Labor Becoming Obsolete?" The live show, beamed over Satcom I, featured a panel discussion of the effects of multinational corporations on the American labor force. During a one-hour phone-in period, more than 2,000 cable viewers in forty-two states called collect with questions for panelists.

The most conspicuous example of cable using satellite to reach beyond the status quo was provided by the nonprofit Cable Satellite Public Affairs Network, which beamed live gavel-to-gavel coverage of the House of Representatives starting in March 1979.* Despite the complaints of House Speaker Tip O'Neill, who claimed that representatives were making speeches chock-full of their constituents' names to an empty chamber after the day's legislative business was over, C-SPAN quickly signed up more than 450 cable systems reaching 5 million homes in all fifty states. The system, created by twenty-three cable operators who raised $400,000 to build an "uplink" to the satellite, charged each participating system one cent per subscriber per month to

*The feed C-SPAN transmitted was provided by the House's camera system. The networks wanted to use their own crews, but the House refused to allow other cameras to cover its proceedings.

cover operating expenses. At the end of 1979, the network planned to expand its service by covering question-and-answer sessions between government officials and thousands of high school students visiting Washington from around the country.

Ted Turner, the flamboyant owner of WTBS Atlanta (formerly WTCG), the nation's first and most successful satellite-transmitted superstation, promised to give news on cable perhaps its most important boost ever with the announcement that he intended to launch the Cable News Network. Scheduled to start up in June 1980, it was supposed to be a national twenty-four-hour all-news operation including a "full network-quality live newscast" and ten minutes of national commercials in each hour. The centerpiece of the day was a prime-time, two-hour newscast from 8:00 to 10:00 P.M. Eastern Time and 5:00 to 7:00 P.M. West Coast Time to be co-anchored by former CBS correspondent Daniel Schorr from Washington with additional help from Atlanta. Also planned were financial news live from Wall Street, regional and national weather, a half-hour sports program at 11:00 P.M., commentaries by columnists Rowland Evans and Robert Novak, *60 Minutes*-type magazine features, in-depth interviews, and a variety of lighter features, including medical notes from Dr. Neil Solomon, psychological advice from Dr. Joyce Brothers, and horoscopes by astrologer Jeane Dixon.

By the fall of 1979, Turner had signed up cable systems with a total of more than a million subscribers to receive the Cable News Network over RCA's $20 million Satcom III satellite, which was launched in December and, to the chagrin of cable operators, malfunctioned and disappeared in space. RCA guaranteed

Turner that his news network would be carried on Satcom I on schedule. But the controversial Georgian still had to snare the 7½ million subscribers necessary to get the project off the ground.

Turner, better known as the owner of the Atlanta Braves and Hawks and for winning the America's Cup yacht race, had previously surprised over-the-air broadcasters by coming up with the novel concept of a superstation. Starting in December 1976, he had bounced the signal from his Atlanta station off a satellite to cable operators who were willing to pay on a per-home-served basis. When the FCC eliminated its rule limiting the number of distant signals that cable operators could import in late 1978, the door was opened for other middlemen to pick up independent local stations' programming and market it nationwide. By mid-1979, the signals of four stations—WTBS Atlanta, WGN-TV Chicago, KTVU-TV San Francisco-Oakland, and WOR-TV New York—were being distributed to cable systems. The stations received no payment, but theoretically they could hike their advertising rates by claiming a much wider audience.

While superstations had no significant impact on over-the-air news operations, they were part of an explosion of technological developments that collectively had the potential to change the entire structure of broadcasting—and broadcast journalism with it. Over-the-air broadcasters were already taking advantage of satellite. The Public Broadcasting Service and National Public Radio had switched completely to satellite feeds. One hundred forty-six public TV stations had earth stations in mid-1979 and were sharing news reports from one another, as well as from Visnews, the CBC, the BBC, and Reuters through the daily exchange feed coordinated by WGBH Boston.* Forty-two commercial stations also had satellite-receiving dishes, and more were planning to build them. Group W, convinced by the Three Mile Island near-catastrophe that its five stations needed to be able to share live news reports, committed $3 million to a hookup through Western Union's satellite. Storer Broadcasting spent $400,000 to install receiving dishes to be used primarily by the news departments at its seven TV stations. The Post-Newsweek stations agreed to build earth stations to receive programs from Viacom Enterprises over Satcom I, and the Mutual Broadcasting System went ahead with its plan to distribute its radio programs by satellite.

Most significant of all, NBC announced at its affiliate convention that it intended to switch completely to satellite distribution by 1983. It asked RCA, Western Union, and AT&T to submit bids for building the system, while ABC asked the three common carriers to come up with more limited proposals for satellite distribution of its programs to Central and Mountain Zone stations. CBS was studying the possibilities but still believed it was less costly to transmit most of its programming through telephone land lines. Meanwhile, the network news operations had already increased their use of satellites.

A few wealthy individuals in remote areas had installed earth stations on their property so they could receive satellite signals direct.* While direct satellite-

*WGBH added a packaged fifteen-minute news program to the daily exchange feed beginning on December 3, 1979.

*Neiman-Marcus of Atlanta featured a $36,500 receiving system as the lead item in its Christmas catalog. But the price of a home earth station was dropping fast. R. B. Cooper, publisher of *Coop's Satellite Digest* of Arcadia, Oklahoma, claimed that a full station to-home receiving was still a luxury item in 1979, the Communications Satellite Corporation (Comsat) unveiled an ambitious plan to offer a complete satellite-to-home subscription TV system at a reasonable cost by 1983. It was hoping to install small earth stations in homes for around two hundred dollars, half what it cost to put in a fancy over-the-air antenna in greater New York City.

The pace at which advanced technology had become feasible and economical was staggering. Video cassette tape recorders and video disks were already available. An information system called Teletext, which gave a viewer access to constantly updated printed information at the push of a button, was being tested over KMOX-TV St. Louis, KSL-TV Salt Lake City, and public station KCET-TV Los Angeles. Fiber optics, a conduit made of finely pulled strands of glass, promised to open up hundreds of channels to cable viewers. Warner's Qube system was already offering 125 channels in its bid for New York's cable franchises in 1979. And further down the line were computerized digital information systems like General Telephone and Electronics' Viewdata and UPI's NewsShare, which would allow subscribers to call up on their TV screens newspaper pages, classified ads, catalogs, restaurant menus, flight schedules, and a variety of other printed materials. The mind-boggling prospect of home information centers complete with computer terminals, video cassette machines, two-way communication, satellite receiving stations, video games, and six-foot-high TV screens with multiple images had become real. Alvin

---

could be sold for $3,000 and that hobbyists had installed them in their homes for as little as $500 in parts.

Toffler, author of *Future Shock,* said, "We're not talking about *watching* the set any more. We're talking about making use of it."

Ralph Nader wrote:

> Those communications satellites high in the sky are not simply objects of wonder; they are the harbingers of a dazzling abundance of instant communications, which could revolutionize the adage that "information is the currency of democracy."
>
> Instead of being mere recipients of what a few large communications companies beam to them, citizens can become active participants in the communications process.

But Nader went on to warn:

> None of this is automatic. New technology can only give us the instruments. The imperative to use these tools wisely and democratically comes from an aware and involved people shaping national policy. For this understanding to evolve, a major public education effort is required. And up to now the media has done very little even to inform people about the new communications technology. . . .
>
> Well, Walter Cronkite, why don't you start the ball rolling? You did such an extensive job on the space program that satellites, cable, and related technology should be an easy transition.*

Bert Cowan, former co-director of the Public Interest Satellite Association, told a national audience watch-

*On October 5, 1972, NBC's *Today* had a segment on the future of satellite communications, but since then none of the commercial TV networks has had a show devoted to the new technology.

ing the *MacNeil-Lehrer Report* that he feared the new technologies would do just the opposite of what Nader hoped:

> What I'm concerned about, as not only the technologies but as cable extends and expands, is who's going to get left out of this brave new world of technological systems. . . . I suspect that it's going to be the poor, the remote, the isolated, the rural, because those are the areas that are harder to cable up, those are the areas that are more costly to cable up, and those are the areas that don't have the discretionary income to pay for all of these brave new things.

It was difficult to take such an argument too seriously, since it had once been made against television itself. But FCC Chairman Charles Ferris, in a speech to the Audit Bureau of Circulation, voiced a much more disturbing concern about the new technologies:

> If these new technologies enter our homes, detail our finances, and deliver our mail; if they serve as our burglar and fire alarms; if they can meter our purchases and record the information we choose to retrieve and the entertainment we choose to watch or the government official we choose not to; if they reveal who our friends are and are not and what we say to them—and if they are, most importantly, linked together in one brave new information empire—they can become the vehicle for stripping us of our privacy, our freedom, and our dignity.

Despite these reservations, Ferris remained basically optimistic about the effect that the new technologies would have on broadcasting. He had often stated his view that neither cable nor over-the-air broadcasting had lived up to its promise. Cable, he acknowledged, had been restrained by government regulation, and the regular networks had been stifled by their "mindless pursuit" of mass audiences and the lowest common denominator. With the arrival of the new technologies and less government intrusion, Ferris hoped for greater competition and a blossoming of diversity and originality in programming.

Nervous as they might have been in private, network executives spoke confidently in public about the future of their industry. To those who were proclaiming the imminent end of advertiser-supported network television, CBS's Gene Jankowski replied:

> Ours is a medium that relies on software and service that have their genesis in creativity, a medium with management able to choose the best of both software and service, a medium that has the capability of risking large capital investments on program development. Therefore, I predict that commercial broadcasting—that CBS and its network and affiliate relationship—are well prepared to exist as well in the future as today.
>
> It's that network pride of programming that convinces me that no matter what the future holds in terms of technology of distribution, no matter whether we have seven or seventy channels available, the network and affiliate partnership approach to broadcasting will be with us for a long time to come.

NBC President Fred Silverman assured his network's affiliates that commercial broadcasting would "continue to be America's first choice." He pointed to an NBC study showing that in 1988 the commercial share of household TV viewing would remain at close to 90 percent. "That suggests that the impact of any one of the alternative program sources will not decrease our audience," declared Silverman, "but will increase the number of hours each household spends watching all television services. . . . Many of the new services will themselves develop into sound businesses and will provide new challenges to our creativity and resourcefulness. But they will not make our kind of free over-the-air television less important."

This kind of bravado aside, there were indications that audiences were not particularly thrilled with network fare. A *Washington Post* poll showed that 53 percent of those surveyed—the highest figure ever recorded—watched less television in 1979 than five years before. Viewers said they were frequently disappointed in the programming they saw. And more than one third of those interviewed said they would be willing to pay more than $80 a year for alternatives to present TV fare.

Thus, it surprised no one that the big broadcasting companies were hedging their bets on the future of their own industry by producing programming for alternative technologies. While Fred Silverman emphasized to his affiliates that NBC was totally committed to broadcasting and would not invest in software for other technologies, he neglected to mention that RCA, NBC's parent company, had already done so years before with the development of the SelectaVision home videodisk, which was scheduled for marketing at $500 a set in 1981. ABC, wanting to get in early on a potentially lucrative new market, created a division to develop programming for cable, video disks, cassettes, and other technologies. CBS announced that it would embark on programming for videodisks that were compatible with RCA's systems. Most of the software contemplated consisted of entertainment and sports, but a notable exception was a monthly program entitled *The Magazine of the Air,* which CBS News already provided for Continental Airlines flights. Anchored by Douglas Edwards, the forty-five-minute videotape was made up of feature stories culled from daily CBS News broadcasts.

How the technological revolution would ultimately affect the networks seemed uncertain at best. If network profits declined, it was certainly possible that news budgets might be cut back drastically. But most commentators and executives thought it more likely that the news divisions would come out on top when the dust settled. For one thing, news programs like *60 Minutes* were already high in the ratings competitions and climbing steadily upward. A survey commissioned by the National Cable Television Association confirmed what cable operators suspected: News was the least vulnerable kind of programming on television. Sixty-one percent of those interviewed expressed a high level of satisfaction with the news and documentaries they saw on TV, and only 12 percent expressed a low level of satisfaction. By contrast, only 45 percent were highly satisfied with specials, sports events, and movies; only 23 percent with entertainment shows; and only 18 percent with children's programs. The new technologies could obviously gain audiences more easily with alternative programming in these other areas than they could with rival news operations.

Far from the obligation that it was once considered, the network news operation was now referred to by executives as the crucial centerpiece of broadcasting's strategy to ward off its rivals. NBC's Fred Silverman boasted:

> Most certainly, no other service can begin to match the network news organizations, which commit more than 300 million dollars each year to bring worldwide coverage into every American home.
>
> Our challenge is to take this incredible service and make it better. At NBC, we think the most important long-term changes we can make will be in the area of news.
>
> We have something unique, something none of the new technologies will ever have—a professional staff of 1,000 journalists with the ability to transmit world events into every living room in the country.
>
> We have this, moreover, at a time when our world has never been more complicated or more difficult to understand. We intend to search for ways to make television more responsive to the public's need for information, more helpful in sorting out the complications of their lives.
>
> It is the most exciting challenge we face and the one, I believe, that is going to change the face of television.

Richard Wald, former president of NBC News and now number two at ABC News, and Reese Schonfeld, head of Ted Turner's upstart Cable News Network, both predicted that the commercial networks would place more emphasis on news as the alternative technologies provided a greater variety of attractive entertainment programming. Bill Leonard, president of CBS News, speculated on what might happen:

> I suspect that we will be in the 24-hour news business in television. Maybe there'll be four basic news broadcasts a day—the evening news, the afternoon news, the morning news, and the late-night news, repeated in half-hour or hour cycles, or shorter cycles, or updated constantly throughout these cycles. Perhaps the evening news with tomorrow's Walter Cronkite would consist of six editions, the poor fellow. And we would constantly be updating that broadcast while at the same time the late-night news production team would be going to work, and they would have their six-hour watch. That's just one of the things that I suspect is going to happen.

Leonard could also envision a day when the new technologies might make First Amendment distinctions between broadcasting and print irrelevant:

> We are rapidly approaching the time when you will not be able to differentiate between a print journalist, a radio journalist, or a television journalist. . . . If you're wired into cable in your particular city or town, you know that there are channels where print is coming out of that television set. Are the people who prepare that material print journalists? Are they television journalists? If audio is added to a print display, are they radio journalists? . . . I will bet you that the time will come when it will be so difficult to differentiate between them that the problem of First Amendment rights for print journalists being almost absolute and First Amendment rights for electronic journalists being much more limited will disappear—because the

proposition that there is a difference will become preposterous.

On the local station level, several news directors who responded to the DuPont-Columbia Survey felt threatened by the arrival of the new technologies. Their greatest fear was that satellite networks and superstations beaming in a wide variety of programming on cable systems would make the local over-the-air broadcaster obsolete. While these intruders could not compete with local news operations, they could potentially outbid broadcasters for important syndicated entertainment fare, snatch a large part of their audience, and cut station profits. If that happened, according to this scenario, management would sacrifice news budgets and desperately throw all available resources into their sagging entertainment shows. "I believe that many stations will drop news if deregulation goes through, because they won't be able to economically compete with some of the new technologies," wrote one gloomy news director from Saint Joseph, Missouri. Another news director, from Seattle, added, "I think local television stations that don't have a commitment to local programming, but act as repeaters of network fare, are in real trouble in the future. . . . Stations that do not . . . produce programming that will offer alternatives . . . telling viewers about the immediate world around them . . . will lose their reason for existence."

But a large majority—83 percent—of the news directors responding to the survey seemed confident that local news operations that offered a unique service to their communities would not suffer because of the new technologies. "I do not see local audiences abandoning their demand for local coverage of local events and people by a television news operation based in that particular area," commented a TV news director from Moline, Illinois. "I see nothing but growth for local news as it is presently constituted."

Many of the local news directors actually welcomed the new technologies and were eager to use them in their operations:

> I think the new technologies are going to improve coverage of the news. . . . Portable satellite up-links will cause stations to form regional coalitions to beam important, same-day information throughout the region. Local newscasts will not have to rely on only the stories they can gather in their local area. They will be able to use "important" stories more regularly and better inform their viewers.
>
> *Seattle, Washington*

> I believe the opening of superstations and more live broadcasting will only serve to spark even more live news coverage by the commercial stations. The prime-time entertainment schedule may be affected, but I believe the news will not be adversely influenced.
>
> *Dallas, Texas*

> We view electronic proliferation in our area as something to be welcomed, rather than as a threat. Small earth stations are beginning to pipe TV network news into many villages we serve. Great! Every little bit helps.
>
> *Nome, Alaska*

> As far as radio is concerned, the new technology can only help by expanding source material. Broadcasters should view any such advances as a

plus and not a threat. Just because a news item is relayed through a satellite instead of phone lines doesn't make it competition. And I don't believe radio listeners will gravitate toward any future radio superstations, because they won't be able to identify with the particular community a listener resides in. An Atlanta radio station simply can't satisfy the information needs of Chicago listeners.

Chicago, Illinois

The technologies have been of great benefit to us. Use of the inexpensive PBS satellite has allowed us to easily surpass our commercial colleagues in Washington coverage. In fact, we have become a superstation of sorts. When especially interesting Washington guests have appeared on our program via satellite, we've alerted our sister stations in Texas, and some of them have picked up the Washington segment of the broadcast for their own use. Also, we're able to easily broadcast statewide via satellite when we find a subject of state interest.

Dallas, Texas

Several other stations, both commercial and noncommercial, reported that they had used the satellite effectively to cover such varied events as the funerals of two popes in Rome, the New York Yankees training camp in Florida, the death of John Wayne in Los Angeles, and the Ted Bundy murder trial in Miami. And new possibilities for using the satellite were being planned. For instance, the Pacifica Foundation, parent organization of listener-sponsored radio stations in Berkeley, Los Angeles, Houston, New York, and Washington, was researching the feasibility of a nationally syndicated, independently produced nightly newscast.

Whether news directors made use of the new technologies or merely responded to the challenge offered by them, local newscasts were bound to change. There were several directions news directors suggested that local newscasts could go to compete successfully in a diversified video marketplace:

> Local news formats, especially in small markets such as ours, must become more analytical than informational. Cable systems, for example, will be able to broadcast entire speeches and public meetings live. Viewers will no longer be satisfied with capsules of what happened there after they have seen it in its entirety. Local reporters will be required to provide background, interpretation, and projecting of future consequences related to such events.
>
> *Hagerstown, Maryland*

> The cable counterprogramming of entertainment shows opposite traditional news hour programs is likely to force a change in the traditional 6 P.M. or 11 P.M. news blocks. Larger news blocks spread over non-traditional news times may result, or in the opposite direction, move towards softer magazine-style news programs to compete with entertainment shows but then enforced throughout the broadcast day with short hard-news summaries.
>
> *Buffalo, New York*

> Local TV news as we know it must cover more pictorially and in more detail individual communities within their viewing area. The analogy is the suburban daily or weekly covering what the big-city newspapers don't, to give a station more local identity. Under the present profit motivation the foregoing is unlikely. The management will com-

pete as they have for years—in entertainment, from where TV was born.

Kansas City, Missouri

We must begin to rethink the idea of news packaged in hour and 90-minute chunks. We should start to think about expanded news breaks during entertainment programming, live inserts when news breaks, different ways of handling reports from the field.

Seattle, Washington

As the 1980s began, it was clear that the technological revolution in communications was already having an effect on local and network news operations across the country. The impact would undoubtedly be felt more with time, but whether it would ultimately improve the quality of broadcast journalism or replace it was a matter of conjecture. It had the potential to do either. As a TV news director from Provo, Utah, wrote, "The new electronic technologies cannot be classified as completely good or completely bad for broadcast journalism. . . . The real problem comes down to the performance of the individual station."

Part III:

Reports

Three Mile Island
by Carolyn Lewis

It was a story like no other story before it: an eerie, compelling blend of high technology, confused experts, White House intervention, and the threat of an unfamiliar and impalpable human disaster. It was a story difficult enough to understand and report for those few with a working knowledge of nuclear reactors, and difficult enough to translate into the print medium. But the March 28 accident at Three Mile Island offered an even greater test of the ingenuity and professionalism of broadcasters.

Broadcasting is a medium that has its own inner logic: brevity, simplicity, the quick summary, the vivid picture. By its nature it is impressionistic, and thus it has limited capacity to deal with highly complex and technical material.

And yet, as the events at Three Mile Island began to impress themselves on the public consciousness, it was to radio—that most immediate and easily accessible of the media—that the public turned most often.

According to a survey by Michigan State University's Professor Stanley Brunn, 56 percent of local residents in Dauphin, Lancaster, and York counties of Pennsylvania first heard of the accident through local radio. Another poll, by Dr. Martin H. Smith of Franklin and Marshall College, showed 56 percent of local residents citing radio as *the major* source of their information about the accident. For Middletown Mayor Robert Reid, radio was also a first source of news about the seriousness of the situation at Three Mile Island, information that conflicted with the soothing murmurs he had been receiving from the utility itself.

In his May 19 testimony before the President's Commission on the Accident at Three Mile Island, Reid said that on the morning of March 28 an official of the utility, Metropolitan Edison, "assured me that no radioactive particles had escaped and no one was injured." He went on, "I felt relieved and relaxed. I said, 'There's no problem.' Twenty seconds later I walked out of my office and got in my car and turned the radio on. The announcer said to me that there were radioactive particles released. Now, I said, gee whiz, what's going on here?"

Reid then testified that at four o'clock that afternoon the same utility official phoned him to say he wanted to update his earlier conversation. Reid continued, "I said, 'Are you going to tell me that radioactive particles were released?' He said, 'Yes.' I said, 'I knew that twenty seconds after I spoke to you on the phone.' "

Not all radio news people in the area were prompt to alert the public to the seriousness of the accident. At WSBA in York County, News Director Ed Wickenheiser learned about it before 7:30 A.M., but he decided not to release the information at that time. The first local station to break the news was a top-40 music outlet in Harrisburg, WKBO, at 8:25 A.M., four hours and twenty-five minutes after the reactor scrammed at Three Mile Island.

While officials and the public were turning to radio for prompt and accurate information during the crisis, the small local stations were ill-prepared for the job. To them, entertainment and commercials were the bread-and-butter of existence. As a staff report to the President's commission put it, "News [was] just a sideline." Thus, the small radio staffs, most without any journalistic expertise to speak of, were strained to the limits by the challenge of Three Mile Island. Schooled in the art of "rip and read" news, they had insufficient skilled manpower to go out and actually cover the breaking story.

What many of the stations did was make drastic changes in their programming. For example, Steve Liddick, news director of WCMB in Harrisburg, said that his normally soft-rock music station "clearly became an all-news station for more than a week." And Mike Pintek, news director of top-40 station WKBO, said that his station "stopped everything whenever there was an update on the TMI story." In addition, according to the staff report of the President's commission, five local stations carried the Nuclear Regulatory Commission press conferences live from Middletown, as well as Governor Richard Thornburgh's press briefings from Harrisburg. One station, WCMB, ran telephone call-in programs to answer citizens' questions, although the station did not have available anyone expert enough to give substantive answers.

Much later, long after the crisis was over, other radio stations (notably KYW in Philadelphia) produced intelligent and probing retrospective documentaries on Three Mile Island. But it was during the crisis, when citizens were hungry for the latest and best news, that radio truly came into its own.

The challenge to television was of a different character. Television, with its double whammy of the spoken word and pictures from the scene, had enormous power to shape the public perception of the event. Who can forget the somber words of Walter Cronkite on the night of March 28—"It was the first step in a nuclear nightmare"—or the grim faces of reporters positioned before the cooling towers of the facility, or the frightened appearance of local citizens, who blamed everything from "a metallic taste in the mouth" to dying cattle on the mysterious goings-on at Three Mile Island.

Ironically, the huge cooling towers that became the most visible and ever-present symbol of the troubles at Three Mile Island are actually one of the least fearsome features of a nuclear power plant. The towers hold no radioactive material but instead are used to cool the water used in the plant, to reduce the level of thermal pollution when the water is finally dumped into the river. If anything, the towers represent a friendly pro-environment presence. And yet, with little else available to use as a picture, television reporters almost always used the towers as a backdrop for their stand-ups and thus helped to turn the innocent edifices into symbols of something dangerous and forbidding.

The presence of the media in large numbers lent credence to the local apprehension that something very dangerous was happening there. Small places like Middletown and Goldsboro are hardly likely to attract so many representatives from the national media unless there is big trouble. But while print reporters can also be intrusive in the life of a small community, nothing was quite as omnipresent as the television camera.

In its search for "local color," television made network stars of the most vocal and available characters, prodding them to tell the world about their fears, to put into words what was often groundless and without shape. As it happened, there was not enough radiation released at Three Mile Island to cause the troubles aired by the citizens interviewed, but the fact that their complaints were heard and seen on television somehow gave them validity. What should have been handled in a sober and rational fashion became something of a Disney World, where what was real could not be separated from what was fantasy.

But to be fair, one reason for the strong reliance on local color for news stories was that official sources on the accident itself were confusing and often unintelligible. Right from the start, the experts were not sure what was happening at Three Mile Island, and the utility spokesmen tried to downplay the seriousness of the event, even when they should have known better.

The confusion began with the misuse of two terms of vital concern to public health and safety. In the earliest hours of the crisis, there was a "site emergency." That meant that there was an above-normal release of radioactivity on-site at Three Mile Island. Then, at a little past 7:30 A.M., the utility declared a "general emergency." That meant that the radioactive emissions had extended outside the bounds of the nuclear reactor gates and could affect the people beyond.

A general emergency obviously has important consequences for local authorities and local citizens. Yet local officials admit they did not understand the term. Eleven hours after the emergency was declared, an official of Metropolitan Edison was still telling Peter Hackes of NBC radio that there was only a site emergency. Even early press releases from the Nuclear Regulatory Commission failed to specify that Three Mile Island involved a general emergency and therefore a potential danger to the public.

The problem was compounded by the failure of the utility and the NRC and, later, state officials, adequately to inform local officials about the true nature of the situation. In his testimony before the President's Three Mile Island commission, the mayor of Lancaster, Albert Wohlsen, said, "We felt that we were completely in the dark in Lancaster, that our information had to come from the media and the press, and of course, some of that was confusing."

Thus, local officials like Mayor Wohlsen, faced with the possibility of preparing the people for evacuation, received little more useful information from the media than they were receiving from the state or the federal government. Confusion was piled on confusion, and the media that were normally merely observers, outsiders, had now become actors and participants in the event itself.

That the information transmitted to reporters on the scene was unclear, conflicting, and sometimes less than frank is now something of a truism. That the reporters were on the whole unprepared to understand what they were being told is the other side of that coin.

Faced with painful unfamiliarity with terms like core uncovery, fuel rod cladding, millirems, and whole body counts, even print reporters—with their luxuries of ample column inches—blanched and reeled. For television reporters, the challenge was intimidating. How can you make a picture out of something that you can't see, not to speak of something you don't understand? How do you run a "sound bite" of a utility or NRC spokesman who doesn't speak in simple jargonless English? How can you sum up something so subtle and obtuse as "the language of uncertainty" that deals in probabilities? How to be responsible in one's reporting, trying to avoid language and pictures that will create panic—while at the same time telling people what you perceive to be a dangerous truth? And how to do it within the confines of the brevity required in television news?

The demand for brevity was especially troublesome when dealing with news sources that offered conflicting information. Print reporters, on the whole, were able to say who was saying what and what gave that individual his credentials for saying it. But broadcasters tended not to use attribution because of their time restrictions. It takes an extra and valuable eight to ten seconds to give a full title or to explain where a source fits into a larger hierarchy. For example, what a mouthful it would be to identify Robert Bernero as "Assistant Director for Material Safety Standards, Division of Engineering Standards, Office of Standards Development of the Nuclear Regulatory Commission." Broadcast reporters are taught that, in using the spoken word, it is preferable to avoid cluttering news copy with unfamiliar names and titles.

As a result, where conflicting information was being offered by different news sources, television viewers were unable to evaluate or weigh the information properly because they couldn't be sure precisely from where it came.

The time constrictions also hampered television's ability to put the situation in context. This is hard enough to do at the best of times, but in an emergency of such potential danger, and of such unfamiliar and fear-provoking character, this became a serious handicap. For example, it was difficult to explain to a worried local population what the danger to their lives and health was when a puff of 1,200 radioactive millirems was released at the stack over Three Mile Island on Friday, March 30. How do you explain what a millirem is, and relative to what, and what it can do to you, let alone explain that the 1,200 millirems at the stack were generally dissipated before they reached local populations—something even the NRC couldn't figure out at the time?

Troubled by this problem, CBS News hired a radiologist named Harry Astarita to advise and interpret the radiation information passed on from official sources. In spite of Astarita's best efforts, however, even Walter Cronkite committed a boo-boo. On March 29, he said, "Trying to put some perspective on those confusing radiation readings, the expert testimony seems to come out like this: If someone living in the small town of Goldsboro, about a mile west of the power plant, stayed outdoors for twenty-four hours following the accident, he would have received the equivalent of three or four chest X-rays." This statement missed one essential point: that such a person would receive the equivalent of three or four X-rays *per hour,* a dose somewhat more dangerous than the one described by Cronkite.

But broadcasters were not the only ones who goofed in handling information about radiation. While both print and broadcast generally reported accurately the figures they were receiving, all the media failed miserably to put those figures in the kind of context that would help the public understand the risks. Even beyond the complex problem of how to translate such information in a short space of time was the problem of how such reporting would be received at the other end. In truth, almost *any* mention of radiation releases, couched in any kind of contextual language, would create fears among ordinary citizens.

In her testimony before the Three Mile Island Commission, a local citizen, Sandra Rineer, spoke of the "nightmare" she experienced on March 30 and quoted from her diary of that date: "This must be the most horrible day of our lives. I heard the first report of an uncontrolled emission of radiation at nine-thirty A.M. and felt absolute terror for the first time in my life." Nearly hysterical, she said she phoned her husband, who urged her to take their children out of school and to leave. Said Mrs. Rineer, "I tried to be rational. I decided not to panic." But as the ominous reports continued, she picked up her children and fled. Given her unpreparedness to comprehend the significance of those bursts of radiation into the atmosphere, given the confusion of the information she was receiving, and given the failure of all the news media, print and broadcasting alike, to make sense out of what was happening, it is understandable that she should choose the course she did.

What made the story of Three Mile Island unique in the history of the news business was not so much what happened but what might have happened. A flood is something tangible and visible. You can watch the water rising, estimate the time of its arrival, and arrange an evacuation accordingly. There are hurricane warnings and tornado watches, and brush fires in California give some evidence of their threat before they sweep through. But here was something that had never happened before, and for many days, even those who should have known did not know what its consequences would be. Furthermore, reporters were uneasy about their own safety, a nervousness reflected by CBS's Gary Shepard, flying over the cooling towers at TMI to take aerial pictures and wondering, "What the hell am I doing here?" and "I wonder what that stuff is doing to me?"

The first two days were scary enough, but then, on Friday, there were the "uncontrolled" releases of radiation and talk of a possible meltdown and, on Saturday, the reports of a potentially explosive hydrogen bubble inside the reactor. How potential? How explosive? How dangerous? What are the probabilities? When would it happen? Reporters on the scene prodded and pushed, wanting some definition of what might lie ahead. In a deposition to the President's commission, the NRC's Harold Denton, Mr. Carter's designated official spokesman in Harrisburg, complained that reporters were always trying to get him to pin down the what-ifs: "There was a lot of focus on what's the worst that can happen, and I always answered it would be a meltdown. And almost every time you'd have to walk through a meltdown, what does it do and how many people die. And there was not as much focus on the probabilities of a meltdown."

It is interesting that in spite of the claims of media critics that the press "sensationalized" the dangers, the facts do not bear out the charges. In a content analysis of news reports by the elite national and local media (*The New York Times, The Washington Post,* wire services, TV networks, etc.),* prepared for the President's Commission on Three Mile Island, New York University Professor Nadyne Edison and her staff found that the press was particularly cautious in its handling of potential risks. She also found that the television networks were generally more conservative than newspapers and wire services. On the state of the hydrogen bubble, Professor Edison counted 149 total media references, of which 136 were reassuring. Only eight people were quoted as saying the bubble was growing. Five of those statements appeared in newspapers, and three on television.

It was the presence of the bubble, and the possibility that it might block the circulation of coolant water around the damaged reactor core, that led to reports of a potential meltdown. In a Friday press conference in Bethesda, NRC spokesman Brian Grimes was saying that "the risk involved is that the gas would expand, prevent cooling of the core, that we would suffer additional core damage, and with the ultimate risk of a meltdown." Similar statements were made by the NRC's Dudley Thompson. That night, CBS aired a videotape of Grimes using the words "ultimate risk of a meltdown." NBC qualified its report by saying that "the real possibility of a meltdown was very small" and attributed that information to Thompson. ABC said, "There is the possibility though not yet the probability of what is called a meltdown."

By comparison, the next day, *The New York Times*

*The study covered the first five days of the accident and included network evening news programs, morning shows, and specials.

began its major headline with the words "U.S. Aides See a Risk of Meltdown," and *The Philadelphia Inquirer* headline read "Possible 'Meltdown' Feared." *The Washington Post* and *The Los Angeles Times,* however, refrained from using the word "meltdown" in the largest type headline on their front pages. Like their colleagues in the print medium, broadcast reporters were frustrated and often angered by the conflicting information emanating from their news sources.

The first problem was in the reporters themselves. Mike Pintek, news director of WKBO Radio, told the President's commission, "The problem for us locally was that none of us had knowledge of nuclear power and couldn't say who was right." And ABC's Bettina Gregory acknowledged that reporters brought to the story the feeling that "sources are never completely on the level and no amount of information is ever enough information." Thus, at the local and national level, reporters were scrambling for a variety of news sources, and many of those sources proved to be neither knowledgeable nor accurate. So what do you do when your sources disagree and you don't know enough to evaluate their differences? Jim Moyer, morning news anchor of radio station WHP in Harrisburg, said, "We just carried both sides and let the public make up its mind," a solution generally followed by the networks and other local stations as well.

But in an emergency situation like this one, is it fair to the public—does it properly serve its right to know —to simply air both sides? Doesn't such "balance," without adequate evaluation and meaningful context, merely add to the confusion?

An example of the confusion came in the debate over

the possible flammability of the hydrogen bubble inside the reactor vessel. At NRC headquarters in Bethesda, it was believed that the hydrogen bubble could combine with oxygen and reach a point where it could explode. Sources from Bethesda were telling the media just that. But at the site itself, NRC sources were saying it couldn't happen. The three television networks combined used eleven statements on the subject, five saying that an explosion was not possible, six indicating that it was. As it turned out, NRC in Bethesda was wrong: There never was a risk of explosion. Unfortunately, for days on end the confusion of the experts had been reflected in reports by the media, and it was the public that was left to wonder whom to believe.

Having said all that, television and radio made a noble effort to rise to the occasion. Networks put on special reports that attempted to explain—and often succeeded in explaining—what was happening. Radio station personnel worked around the clock to provide a public service. Reporters and technical personnel ignored the possible risks to their own health and safety, while struggling bravely with an unfamiliar technology as well as with a tangle of mixed-up experts and spokesmen.

It was an event like nothing else before it, but it offered a clear lesson for the future: Broadcasters, like print reporters, must find ways to understand the new, complex, and often dangerous technologies like nuclear power *before* the accidents happen, and they must find ways to adapt their medium to the critical demands of complex and technical stories like Three Mile Island.

The First Amendment was designed to serve the public's right to information. In a situation like Three

Mile Island, so fraught with risk of citizen panic and danger to human life, the media shoulder an especially heavy responsibility to tell it right and tell it whole, as well as to tell it fast.

The Burger Court and Broadcasting: An Uneasy Balance

by Tom Goldstein

Chief Justice Warren E. Burger does not like bright lights. For one thing, his eyes are very sensitive, and he says he cannot see his notes when lighting is intense. What is more, for someone who has made such a fuss about how inadequately trial lawyers perform, the Chief Justice comes off surprisingly poorly as a public speaker. He talks in a droning, undramatic voice and does not infuse his speeches with pacing or punch. Finally, Justice Burger places extremely high value on privacy, his own and others.

And so it comes as no great shock that he feels uncomfortable appearing on television. He has delivered an unusually large number of speeches since he was named to the court by President Nixon in 1969, but with few exceptions, the Chief Justice has refused to let television cameras cover these appearances. This has led to friction between reporters and the Justice, and often the confrontation over his not allowing television to record his speech has become the news story, obscuring the subject matter which Justice Burger was addressing.

In the spring of 1979, the Chief Justice, in a particularly shrill statement released by the Supreme Court's public information office, reiterated his policy toward television. Citing "the long tradition of isolation of judges from day-to-day controversy," the statement expressed dismay at the behavior of television reporters who at American Bar Association meetings "as well as elsewhere accosted the Chief Justice in hotel lobbies, on streets, and in other public places, thrusting microphones at him for impromptu press conferences with questions on subjects wholly inappropriate for comment by any judge."

Any claim by reporters, the statement continued, "of a First Amendment right to accost a justice or judge with microphones in public places and private gatherings" ignores what many distinguished jurists have said: "that the First Amendment is a collection of rights, not least of which is the right to be let alone, a principle embedded firmly in American tradition." But if Justice Burger and the Supreme Court are not the best friends of newspapers, magazines, radio, and television, the ten years of the Burger court have been far from an unmitigated disaster for the press. Indeed, the court's record, looked at in the long term, is far more sympathetic to the press than has generally been understood. In the past decade, the court has ruled in more than twenty cases involving freedom of the press. In nearly half, the press has won its argument.

The majority of those cases have dealt with print media, but most of these cases also carry relevance for broadcasters.

The Supreme Court has rejected government efforts to control the content of newspapers, magazines, or broadcast reports, through court orders halting publication or through "gag" orders on participants of trials. But when privacy and press interests collide, the present court has been more receptive to arguments of individual privacy and reputation. For the first time, in the 1970s, arguments were introduced that the First Amendment gives reporters special privileges to withhold information or special rights of access to information, but the Supreme Court has not accepted this line of argument.

Some of these cases involve direct restraints on press access. For example, there have been decisions holding that the press has no special right of access to prison beyond that enjoyed by the public. Other cases involve claims that if journalists have to supply certain evidence, their news sources will dry up.

According to Benno C. Schmidt, Jr., a professor at Columbia University Law School, "No such rights have been recognized by our constitution. In rejecting such claims, the Burger Court is not retreating but refusing to advance into uncharted territory." Professor Schmidt who served as a clerk for Earl Warren, Justice Burger's predecessor, adds, "The strident denunciations of the Burger Court as an enemy of press freedom reflect a gross lack of proportion. The Burger Court is a staunch friend of press freedom when it counts, when freedom over what to publish is in jeopardy."

And there is no doubt that the reactions of the press have been strident. Allan H. Neuharth, president of the American Newspaper Publishers Association, told the group's convention in the spring of 1979 that the Supreme Court "has battered holes in the First Amendment big enough to drive the whole Constitution through."

In its July 9, 1979, issue, *Broadcasting* magazine

spoke sardonically of a series of cases which the press
lost between May 1978 and July 1979 as the Burger
Court's "parting gift to journalism." The headline for
the story was: "Battered by the Hands of the Burger
Court."

One of the cases that raised the most hackles among
the press in the 1979 term was the Herbert decision. In
that 6-to-3 decision, the court ruled that journalists who
are sued for libel must answer questions about what
they were thinking when they prepared their reports.

Writing for the majority, Justice Byron White ruled
that retired Lieutenant Colonel Anthony Herbert, who
had accused the army of covering up reports of civilian
killings in Vietnam, could probe into the "thoughts,
opinions and conclusions" of the producers of CBS' *60
Minutes* in his attempt to prove that the show libeled
him. In pretrial proceedings, Barry Lando, the producer of the Herbert segment, testified for twenty-six
days. He answered innumerable questions about what
he knew or had seen, whom he had interviewed, and
the form and frequency of his communications with
sources. The exhibits included transcripts of his interviews, volumes of reporter's notes, videotapes of interviews, and a series of drafts of the telecast. However,
Mr. Lando refused to answer questions about his "opinions, intent, and conclusions," claiming this was an unwarranted intrusion into the editorial process, and the
United States Court of Appeals for the Second Circuit
backed his contention in a 1977 opinion by Judge Ir-
ving R. Kaufman, a New York City judge who over the
years has issued a series of opinions highly favorable to
the press.

The Supreme Court reversed, but the reversal was
not a clean-cut one. In all, there were five opinions,

each touching on what the reporter's "state of mind" had to be in order to prove libel.

In law, all is not what it appears to be. In the landmark 1964 case, *New York Times* v. *Sullivan,* the Supreme Court held that when the press is sued for libel as a result of its publication or broadcasting of derogatory information about a public official, the First Amendment requires that the official prove both that the report was false and that it was published with "actual malice."

But in *Times* v. *Sullivan,* "actual malice" was not used in its ordinary meaning. Since that case, federal and state courts have ruled that ill will, spite, hatred, hostility, deliberate intention to harm, or even some sinister or corrupt motive are constitutionally insufficient to establish "actual malice." In fact, "actual malice" is not malice at all, and in order to satisfy the standard laid down in *Times* v. *Sullivan,* a plaintiff must prove either actual knowledge that the report is false or a reckless disregard of whether the statements are false.

This all gets very confusing, and sometimes even highly skilled lawyers and judges miss the point. In a dissent in the Herbert case, Justice Potter Stewart claimed that the majority had actually mistaken the meaning of malice. He said that since actual malice has nothing to do with ill will, "the question 'why?' is irrelevant" and liability "ultimately depends upon the publisher's state of knowledge of the falsity of what he published, not at all upon his motivation in publishing it." Therefore, Justice Stewart concluded, "inquiries into a reporter's state of mind are not permissible."

Notwithstanding the confusion of what the case actually meant, the reaction by the press was loud and negative. It also has not subsided much, even though there has been no evidence that sources for reporters have dried up or that aggressive reporting that characterizes a show like *60 Minutes* has been hampered.

In a speech in October 1979, Justice William Brennan, who dissented in part from the Herbert holding, said the reaction of the press to the case was "a virtually unprecedented outpouring of scathing criticism."

The *Washington Star* labeled the decision "judicial Agnewism." The *Miami Herald* said the decision was an example of the court following "its anti-press course into what can only be called an Orwellian domain." The managing editor of the *St. Louis Post-Dispatch* stated that the opinion "has the potential of totally inhibiting the press to a degree seldom seen outside a dictatorial or fascist country."

In his speech, Justice Brennan alluded to a string of "unfortunate examples of inaccurate reporting." Beyond that, he said, "the deepest sources of the press's outrage was I think well captured by William Leonard, president of CBS news." Leonard said that the Herbert decision denied constitutional protection to "the journalist's most precious possession: his mind, his thoughts, and his editorial judgment." But, the justice pointed out, the inquiry into a defendant's state of mind, into his intent, is "one of the most common procedures in the law." Almost all crimes require that some element of the defendant's intent be established. For example, if John kills Judy, that killing can be classified as an accident (if John acted in self-defense) or a murder (if he acted with cold-blooded premeditation), with several gradations in between. The law of contracts rests on intent. So does the law of damages. State of mind can be relevant to questions of fraud and recklessness.

In the area of libel, said Justice Brennan, "it would scarcely be fair to say that a plaintiff can only recover if he establishes intentional falsehood and at the same time to say that he cannot inquire into a defendant's intentions." It is Justice Brennan's view that "reporters will not cease to publish because they are later asked about their state of mind."

The court closed its 1979 term with another confusing and controversial case dealing with the press, and in this instance, said Justice Brennan, the press's criticism was "intelligently and searchingly" presented. Yet, he added, "the impact of the press's quite correct reaction was undercut by the unjustified violence of its previous responses to *Herbert* v. *Lando* and other such cases."

The later case, *Gannett* v. *DePasquale,* dealt with newspapers, but it has important applications for television, especially since more and more states are permitting court hearings to be televised. By a 5-to-4 vote, the court ruled that trial judges had broad discretion to conduct closed criminal proceedings to minimize prejudicial publicity toward a defendant. It is by no means clear whether the court authorized the closing of entire trials or whether its holding was limited to pretrial hearings.

In the months immediately following the filing of that opinion, five justices publicly commented on what they thought the opinion meant, and no two agreed. Chief Justice Burger began the extraordinary series of out-of-court comments by saying that the opinion had generally been misread and applied solely to pretrial hearings. So embedded is the tradition in American jurisprudence that opinions speak for themselves that it is rare for a single justice to speak out once in a decade on what a specific case meant. It is without precedent for five to do so. And they did so without clarifying the central question: whether the decision applied only to pretrial hearings or to entire trials.

It is ironic that, the same year in which the Supreme Court sent a signal that courtrooms can be closed to the public and press at least some of the time, television has enjoyed its greatest success in penetrating the mystique of the courtroom.

Until the early 1960s, there were limited experiments in bringing television into the courtroom, but those attempts ended soon after the conviction of Billie Sol Estes, the flamboyant Texas financier. At his 1962 trial in Smith County, about one hundred miles from Dallas, flashbulbs popped, spotlights glared, and cameras whirred in the courtroom. Three years later, the United States Supreme Court overturned Estes's fraud conviction on the grounds that his televised trial denied him due process of law and subjected him to "a form of mental—if not physical—harassment, resembling a police line-up or the third degree."

But there have been dramatic improvements in television technology since then, and cameras have been designed that are unobtrusive. Now, more than half the states allow cameras in trial or appellate courtrooms on a temporary or permanent basis. Cameras still are not permitted in any courtroom in the federal system, the system that Justice Burger presides over.

The impact of television has gone far beyond those states that permit coverage. For example, portions of the trial of Theodore R. Bundy, who was convicted in the summer of 1979 of murdering two coeds at a Florida State University sorority house, were televised nationally, including those states where cameras are not permitted in courtrooms. The resistance to televised trials is still deep-seated, but there are signs it is weakening. In 1979, leaders of the American Bar Association, whose membership includes about half the country's 500,000 lawyers, barely defeated a motion that would have changed the bar's long-standing opposition to televised proceedings. Once again, though, the bar group seems to be out of step with the mainstream. The summer before, chief justices of the states voted 44 to 1 to open courtrooms to television in some circumstances. And a pair of empirical studies suggest that the more often judges are exposed to televised hearings, the less likely they are to resist opening their courtrooms to cameras.

There seems to be little legitimate argument for keeping cameras out of appellate courtrooms, where the only participants are judges and lawyers. To be sure, at least in the early stages of televising such hearings, judges may ask more questions than they ordinarily do, and lawyers may be on their best behavior. But it is arguable whether these are adequate reasons to close appellate courtrooms to electronic media. Indeed, they may be reasons for encouraging television to come in.

Trials, on the other hand, present trickier problems, and it is at this level that there is presumably the greatest interest in televising proceedings. Such coverage may be in the public's interest, but what about the interests of parties to the lawsuit, or of witnesses, or of jurors?

"It is inevitable that some trial participants will react with great reluctance or even fear to the prospect of having their identities, likenesses, voices, and mannerisms broadcast to a mass television audience," said Lee

Loevinger, a former commissioner of the Federal Communications Commission, at an American Bar Association meeting in the summer of 1979. Loevinger, now a Washington lawyer, favors the televising of trials on the condition that parties, witnesses, lawyers, and jurors be given the right not to be pictured. But such restrictions could create grave—perhaps insurmountable—technical difficulties.

At bottom, what Loevinger was speaking about was the privacy rights of the participants of a trial. Of all the media, television has the greatest capacity for the invasion of an individual's privacy, and in the future it is likely that the law of privacy will be expanded. In the words of Floyd Abrams, who may be the leading press lawyer in the country, the "explosion" of privacy law has become "the single most ominous threat to the First Amendment's guarantee of press freedom."

In the area of privacy, questions of what is proper and what is tasteful are often as significant as issues of what is legal. So far, the Supreme Court has not ruled frequently in this area, but lower courts have.

In 1978, an appellate court in Manhattan ruled that a trespass had been committed, making CBS accountable for damages, when the camera crew of its local station entered an exclusive midtown restaurant without permission and began filming. The restaurant had been cited for violations of the city's health code. There were procedural complexities to the opinion, but in essence the appellate judges seemed particularly disturbed by the manner in which the CBS film crew entered the restaurant.

The opinion quoted in great detail from the trial judge's observation that "from the evidence the jury was entitled to conclude" that the CBS camera crew and its reporter, Lucille Rich, "burst into plaintiff's restaurant in noisy fashion and following the loud commands of the reporter, Rich, to photograph the patrons dining, turned their lights and camera upon the dining room." The trial judge continued, "Consternation, the jury was informed, followed. Patrons waiting to be seated left the restaurant. Others who had finished eating left without waiting for their checks. Still others hid their faces behind napkins or tablecloths or hid themselves beneath tables. (The reluctance of the plaintiff's clientele to be videotaped was never explained, and need not be. Patronizing a restaurant does not carry with it an obligation to appear on television)."

Physical intrusions or trespasses by the press in the course of newsgathering form one type of privacy action. Another privacy action involves an individual's right to sell his or her own name or likeness, and the Supreme Court's last major privacy decision, in 1977, dealt with this issue.

That case involved a "human cannonball," Hugo Zacchini, and by a 5-to-4 vote the court said Zacchini may be entitled to recover monetary damages from a television station which filmed him being projected out of a cannonlike object into a net 200 feet away and then broadcast the entire act, which lasted 15 seconds, on its late-night news show.

While the film clip was being shown, the newscaster's voice-over included these words: "Believe me, although it's not a long act, it's a thriller . . . and you really need to see it in person . . . to appreciate it."

Does it make any difference, in a constitutional sense, that the performance was broadcast as part of the station's routine news program rather than as commercial entertainment? A dissenter to the Supreme Court majority, Justice Lewis Powell, Jr., argued the station was protected from a "right of publicity" or "appropriation" suit because the film was used for a routine portion of a regular news program. But distinguishing "news" from "commercial" broadcasts is a fragile business—probably too fragile to rest great constitutional issues on.

The Zacchini case has become fodder for law review writers, who argue that the decision does little to clarify the relationship between the First Amendment and the right of publicity. What disturbs many of the most thoughtful commentators is not so much in whose favor the court decides an issue, but that when it does decide, as in the Zacchini case, the decisions are confusing and fail to set sufficiently clear standards.

It seems fair to speculate that media cases will continue to occupy a significant portion of the Supreme Court's calendar. But even for an institution theoretically as wedded to tradition and precedent as the Supreme Court, the past offers little guidance to the future. In the 1970s, there was an uncommon stability to the membership to the court. There were few changes in personnel. Even still, the court, at times, had difficulty setting forth a coherent philosophy. At the end of 1979, five of the justices, including the Chief Justice, were more than seventy-one years old, and some had been gravely ill. There is no mandatory retirement age for justices, but it seemed likely that the winner of the 1980 presidential election would have an almost unparalleled opportunity to appoint new justices, shaping the court and, by extension, its philosophy.

The Picture from Abroad
by Jan Stone

Don Hewitt, executive producer of *60 Minutes*, remarked recently, "There was a time when CBS's foreign coverage could hold its own with any news organization in the world. I'm not sure about that now—not about CBS or any other network."

NBC's John Chancellor was even more apprehensive:

> Foreign coverage has changed considerably. When I went into the foreign press corps for NBC, we called it "the NBC Foreign Service." Then, the reporting was more thoughtful. We had more time.
>
> Now I am troubled with the way we cover foreign news. It is less thoughtful. American coverage of foreign affairs is declining—and that's dangerous.

By the end of the 1970s several factors—new technologies, inflation, editorial choices reflecting waning public interest in foreign affairs, and increased press censorship abroad—had changed network foreign news coverage from the days Don Hewitt recalled, "when CBS News had Schoenbrun, Smith, Hotellet, Sevareid, Burdett, and others." That was the same era when correspondents based in foreign bureaus were, as John Chancellor called them, "area specialists."

Foremost in causing the changes were a number of technological developments in communications as well as in transportation. Their emergence created a demand for more visual stories, delivered with greater speed than ever before. The tools—designed to aid foreign correspondents in their work—were perceived by some as a giant Pandora's box, creating new problems for correspondents, preventing them from doing their jobs as thoroughly and thoughtfully as they might, transforming the correspondent from area specialist to time-pressured, globe-trotting generalist. Among the items were:

1. The satellite. In 1969, the first DuPont-Columbia Survey reported that "network use of satellites, although still relatively slight, had jumped from 40 hours in 1965 to 666 hours in 1968." A decade later, commercial network use of the Intelsat-system satellites for the year 1978 had climbed to approximately 1,400 hours. In 1969, one regular satellite feed from abroad—carrying reports from Vietnam—was transmitted each day to New York, along with an occasional feed from Europe. By 1979, as many as five to seven overseas feeds—containing up to twenty separate stories for editors to screen—were beamed daily to each network. And the number of working Intelsat earth station antennas dotting the globe, transmitting and receiving signals, had increased from a handful in 1969 to 258 in 1979. Yet, at the same time, the space available to foreign news on the air did not grow substantially larger.

(For a discussion of special foreign coverage in 1978–79, including events in Iran, see chapter 5.)

2. Electronic news gathering (ENG). In 1969, film was used to cover all foreign stories. By 1979, more than 80 percent of all foreign stories filed by network correspondents were recorded by electronic equipment. Stories gathered by video cameras and tape required no developing time; they could be edited immediately and transmitted as soon as satellite feed time was available. ENG's advantage over film was its ability to deliver late-breaking stories in time for the evening news. ABC's director of television news coverage, Stan Opotowsky, spoke enthusiastically about that capability. "In Nicaragua, for example, there are no film labs. We would have had to shoot our stories and ship the film out. But with ENG, we shot and broadcast the same day. ENG has made it possible to cover stories quickly, stories we could not have covered in the past."

But Opotowsky conceded that ENG, particularly in combination with satellite transmission, posed some problems. Because the networks edit and transmit on New York time, reporters overseas worked all day on their local time to cover a story and then stayed up most of the night to edit and transmit; the next morning, the cycle began again. Hardest hit were correspondents in the Middle and Far East. "When there's a continuing story—two or three weeks long—we will double staff and relieve people," Opotowsky said. "The problem then is that you lose the journalistic continuity of the story." Opotowsky mentioned another effect electronic coverage had on stories filed from abroad. "In film days," he said, "foreign correspondents had to 'pad' with background when they couldn't get that day's news on the air. Now they use background only when it's necessary, no longer as a cover-up." The point can well be made that those backgrounders added depth to developing stories.

3. The telephone. Even the technology of the telephone made conspicuous strides. In 1969, all overseas calls were connected through a series of operators subject to delay and human error; in 1979 New York editors could direct-dial to seventy-five nations overseas.

4. The airplane. Lastly, the increase in frequency and ease of air travel made its contribution, enabling correspondents to jump from one location to another as a matter of routine.

The technological revolution placed a premium on speed in the gathering and delivery of more stories from abroad. As John Chancellor observed, "Now, foreign reporting is shallower. There is . . . a greater emphasis on young people with good legs." Foreign correspondents in 1979, according to Chancellor, were "firemen, rushing to the fire."

The nature of the news bureau, too, had changed. Bureaus were less often places for a correspondent to develop an area expertise; more and more they had become mere "jumping-off points." Despite a 25-percent increase in the number of network television foreign bureaus during the decade (up from thirty-five to forty-four by October 1979), eleven of them were not assigned permanent correspondents. In addition, the locations of some bureaus had been chosen not because they were centers of political activity but because they were centers for airline connections. NBC, for example, maintained a bureau in Frankfurt rather than Bonn, explained a network official, because "it's the O'Hare Airport of Europe." And ABC News's most important Latin America bureau was in Miami—because more flights to Central and South America locations flew from there than from any Latin American city. Foreign correspondents traveled extensively, and one of their chief complaints was of wasted time in the air and in airports. Don Dunkel, NBC's vice-president for news operations, said, "It can take two to three hours just to clear an airport sometimes in certain nations. The reporter can totally miss the fire."

As correspondents raced to get their stories, the network news organizations spent the decade trying to keep up with inflation. The cost of goods and services had doubled between January 1968 and December 1978. Abroad, the situation was worse as the dollar's value in many foreign markets dropped from day to day. *Variety* reported that each network was spending between $23 and $26 million a year to cover foreign news, double the amounts they had spent ten years before.

But the expansion seemed much less impressive in the light of total network programming budgets, tagged at $2 billion for 1978: Only 15 percent of that figure ($300 million) went to news programming. Given foreign news coverage's 25-percent share of the overall network news budgets, its piece in the entire programming pie was just under 4 percent.

Nor could the time allowed foreign news on the evening newscasts, except in time of crisis, justify a much larger expenditure. From July 1978 through June 1979 20 to 25 percent of the network evening newscasts were devoted to foreign news. *60 Minutes'* foreign allotment averaged 20 percent, while the other two network magazine shows, *20/20* and *Prime Time Sunday,* managed less than half of that.

Although some of the most thorough and useful foreign reporting was done in network documentaries and special reports, the season of 1978–79 saw a total of only six prime-time hours on the commercial networks devoted to overseas subjects.

The dearth of foreign news on the air in times of comparative peace perhaps had more to do with editors' perceptions of public interest than it did with technology or inflation. America's attention had turned inward after the Vietnam War—that was at least one interpretation given the result of the Overseas Press Club's survey in 1975 that reflected a drop in American correspondents abroad. As editors turned to problems of energy and inflation, developments and changes in the traditional foreign powers and the emergence of other nations between 1969 and 1979* garnered comparatively little attention.

A survey of one month in 1979 showed that the TV networks' evening newscasts carried a combined total of six items about South America—four of which dealt with Venezuelan oil supplies and prices. Commented NBC's Don Dunkel, "I think the interest in South America on the part of the American population is just about nil. Now, Central America is a different story." At the time Dunkel commented, the Nicaraguan revolution was in full flower. Stan Opotowsky described the process of story selection: "Our motive is to inform a clientele public. . . . We go out, get news, and sell it to the people who want to see it." Dunkel added, "If our newscaster opened tonight with the great truth about Ethiopia, somebody—probably in Ethiopia—might be delighted. But that would be the end of our newscast!"

*In that decade twenty-five new nations joined the United Nations.

Coverage of Africa rated slightly higher than that of South America during the same month. For all of black Africa—an area containing more than thirty nations and 350 million people—the networks carried thirty-one items; more than half of them, however, dealt exclusively with the Uganda-Tanzania conflict.

Such numbers added fuel to the arguments made by critics of Western coverage of developing nations. Former UPI correspondent Nicholas King, in his book *The Third World Has a Point,* insisted that the Western press paid too little attention to "health programs, housing developments, [and] cultural maturity" in developing nations and too much to "bloodshed, unrest, poverty, disease, murder, and general violence." And *London Times* reporter Rosemary Righter wrote in her book, *Improving Global News Flow,* "One difficulty for the Western press is that its very code of objectivity, accuracy, etc., lends itself to spot reporting, to the thing which can be 'pegged.' But what is happening in the Third World has much more to do with things that didn't start yesterday and won't stop tomorrow."

Beyond the changes in coverage wrought by technology, inflation, and editors' predilections for visual stories and their general disregard for two continents, another problem—that of censorship—impeded the presentation of foreign news to the American public. Although censorship was not a new problem, its scope had widened in the 1970s, making much coverage difficult if not downright impossible. Richard Salant told *Broadcasting* magazine that in the area of world press freedoms things were going "very badly. Very, very badly. We lose ground almost every day. Progressively more countries are curtailing press freedoms."

In 1978, more than eighteen governments harassed,

arrested, expelled, or denied visas to foreign correspondents, according to the Zurich-based International
Press Institute. And in the first half of 1979, no fewer
than eleven incidents of press violations against foreign
correspondents were reported by the IPI and *The New
York Times.*

Censorship continued to prevail in most of the world.
ABC News's Stan Opotowsky commented on the forms
of censorship that confronted and at times confounded
television journalists overseas:

> Only in Israel do we have a censor who sits and
> says, "You can do this, you can't do that." Every-
> where else, governments censor us differently.
> They censor us by visa: if they want us to get a
> story, we get our visa; if they don't, no visa.
>
> They censor us by customs: we may arrive to do
> a story and they may say that it will take three
> weeks to clear our equipment through customs.
>
> They censor us by access: they may say, "Sure,
> you can come into our country, but the meeting is
> over there, and no reporters are allowed within a
> twelve-block radius of the building—though
> you're welcome to stay at the hotel and go to the
> cocktail lounge."
>
> Ultimately, they censor us by facilities: if we're
> transmitting material from a government-owned
> station—and except in the United States, most sta-
> tions are government-owned—a number of things
> can happen if the government doesn't like the
> story we're sending: a censor will fail to arrive; or
> the building's electricity will mysteriously fail; or
> a tape machine will suddenly break; or the line
> between the station transmission and the ground
> station will fail; or, ultimately, the satellite will fail.
>
> Those kinds of censorship—which the govern-

ments would never admit to—are our biggest problems.

In Uganda, resistance to Western press coverage forced American reporters to "cover" the overthrow of Idi Amin from "observation points" thousands of miles away in Nairobi and Johannesburg. Two other African despots fell from power—President Nguema Biyoto Masie of Equatorial Guinea and Emperor Bokassa I of the Central African Empire—but because American (and other Western) journalists had been expelled long before by those rulers, only sketchy reports trickled to America from Paris.

Other areas of strife in the Third World were covered from great distances because American correspondents could not gain entry. For that reason, American coverage of the Chinese invasion of Vietnam in February 1979 suffered. Only a CBS crew accompanying two members of Congress on a tour of Vietnam at the time of the invasion came close to the action. No Western reporters could enter from China. Bangkok, the intelligence center for Asia, was a nest of gossip and rumors. Refugee reports and press releases and film from the government-controlled news services of China and Vietnam fed to American news media became the chief sources of news for the American public. On February 19, ABC reported from Hong Kong that China was pulling back from the invasion area; CBS reported from Bangkok that Chinese withdrawal was about to take place, and NBC reported in New York that sources in both Washington, D.C., and Peking indicated that a Chinese pullout had begun. All the reports proved inaccurate. For two more weeks, the fighting continued. Anchormen and correspondents noted in newscasts that Chinese authorities were providing no information and that reports of battles and casualties were unconfirmed. On February 23, CBS noted American intelligence reports that Chinese aircraft had bombed sections of Haiphong. Again, the report was incorrect. By the time the networks reported on March 2 and 3 that Chinese officials had announced an imminent withdrawal of their troops, the American public had learned only the barest details about the conflict.

When full-scale fighting erupted in Afghanistan in July 1979, the networks were denied entry visas. Alan Walden, NBC's director of radio news, said at the time, "Clearly there's a story there. It could be the Soviet Union's Vietnam. But even if we could get in, a crew would never get out alive." And so American news media continued watching events in Afghanistan from India and Pakistan until January 1980 when the newly Soviet-supported government allowed U.S. journalists in, only to expel them two weeks later.

Thus, censorship by foreign governments on American network news stories diminished further the number of foreign stories available to the American television news audiences and—where cameras were permitted with restrictions—made stories incomplete, hazy, and speculative. Censorship by the nations of the Third World shrank even more the minimal coverage devoted to them on American television network newscasts.

While a foreign government's disposition toward a free press was ultimately out of the hands of American network news, editorial decisions about the content and scope of news features, documentaries, and magazine segments were not. If the so-called average citizen did not think social unrest in Central America or the development of an African nation had meaning for him or her, it was the task of the networks' news organizations *not* to give in to that notion but rather to show its viewers why and how those events did indeed have an impact on the United States and its citizens. And while inflation posed a problem to foreign editors, a bigger problem was posed by network executives whose budgetary dispensations and time allotments favored entertainment over news. Though technological developments had helped shrink the globe, political developments had expanded it by adding new nations with new problems and needs that were already having an impact on the ever-changing world order—including the United States.

Some Information about the Alfred I. duPont- Columbia University Awards for 1978-79

Each year the awards are based upon research done in conjunction with the annual Alfred I. duPont– Columbia University Survey of Broadcast Journalism. There is no set number of awards, nor are there categories for the awards. Local and network radio, local and network television, as well as syndicated material and the work of independent producers, will be surveyed and considered for awards.

Concerned parties are encouraged to suggest to the jurors examples of broadcast journalism that they feel are particularly worthy of attention. They are also invited to recommend subjects for research.

Suggestions for those wishing to participate:

1. Any person, group, organization, or broadcast station may bring to the DuPont-Columbia jury's attention material dealing with performance—one-time or long-term— in broadcast news and public affairs by an individual, a station, or other institutions.

2. The nomination should include the following particulars: (a) time, date, and call letters of the station carrying the program, (b) the sub-

ject of the program, (c) the reason the program or the individual is being singled out.

3. Tapes and other supporting material should not be submitted unless expressly asked for by the Director.

4. Although our broadcast year runs from July 1 to June 30, nominations may be made throughout the year.

5. Nominations must be postmarked no later than midnight July 2.

6. All materials submitted will become the property of Columbia University.

7. All inquiries and correspondence should be addressed to:

Marvin Barrett, Director
Alfred I. duPont–Columbia University
Survey and Awards
Graduate School of Journalism
Columbia University
New York, NY 10027

Acknowledgments

We are grateful to all those organizations and individuals who have offered us generous assistance in putting together this volume. Unfortunately, it is not possible to list them all. However, we would particularly like to express our gratitude to the news directors and newsmen and women from the networks and individual stations who answered questionnaires, furnished tapes and films, and produced the news and public affairs with which this volume and the Alfred I. duPont–Columbia University Awards are particularly concerned.

We would also like to thank the awards and public information departments of the commercial and public networks, as well as individual radio and television stations, upon whose help, as always, we depended heavily. We are particularly grateful this year to those television and radio critics and the major business advertisers who participated in our research.

Each year the volume of material to be handled in judging the awards and compiling this report increases with a commensurate broadening of reportorial and research chores. My assistant director, Barbara Eddings, once again has been in charge of the formidable logistics involved in this process. Assisting us were Du-Pont Fellow Jan Stone and administrative assistant Dinorah Pineiro.

Thanks are due to our special consultants Harry Arouh and Carolyn Lewis, and to our DuPont screeners.

Again, the reporters of *Variety, Advertising Age, Broadcasting, The New York Times, The Wall Street Journal, Television/Radio Age, TV Guide,* and the *Columbia Journalism Review* furnished both individual insights and continuous coverage of the broadcast scene which were invaluable to the editor and the jurors.

Finally, the network of DuPont-Columbia correspondents across the country has been invaluable in providing those specific insights into local television and radio which are so important a part of the overall picture of broadcast journalism that we hope this book provides.

We would particularly like to thank the trustees of the Alfred I. duPont Awards Foundation, who have supported our expanding activities so generously. We hope that we have succeeded in fulfilling the intentions of the late Jessie Ball duPont in establishing the awards thirty-eight years ago to honor her husband by encouraging the best in broadcast journalism.

Index

Note: Unless otherwise identified, entries in italics denote television or radio series and those in quotation marks denote individual programs.

The decade of the 1970s saw broadcast journalism emerge as the primary news source of 67 percent of the nation—the only U.S. institution whose credibility actually increased rather than dwindled during the period. No longer a perennial sop to Washington regulatory commissions, radio/TV news and public affairs is now a massive, widely successful enterprise—at the same time that the industry stands on the verge of a technological revolution capable of changing the very nature of broadcasting and American life along with it.

The seventh volume in the prestigious series of Alfred I. duPont–Columbia University Surveys of Broadcast Journalism, *The Eye of the Storm* provides a fascinating behind-the-scenes look at the way in which electronic journalists handled the major issues and events of 1978–79: Jonestown and Nicaragua, Three Mile Island and the return of the energy crisis, Skylab and the DC-10,